Why Boredom Matters

Boredom is an enduring problem. In response, schools often do one or both of the following: First, they endorse what novelist Walker Percy describes as a "boredom avoidance scheme," adopting new initiative after initiative in the hope that boredom can be outrun altogether. Second, they compel students to accept boring situations as an inevitable part of life. Both strategies avoid serious reflection on this universal and troubling state of mind. In this book, Gary argues that schools should educate students on how to engage with boredom productively. Rather than being conditioned to avoid or blame boredom on something or someone else, students need to be given tools for dealing with their boredom. These tools provide them with internal resources that equip them to find worthwhile activities and practices to transform boredom into a more productive state of mind. This book addresses the ways students might gain these skills.

Kevin Hood Gary is a professor of education at Valparaiso University. His primary areas of interest include philosophy of education, ethics, and moral formation. He is a co-founder of the North American Association for Philosophy of Education, which provides a hospitable space for scholars working at the intersection of philosophy and educational thought. He recently completed a four-year term as the Richard P. Baepler Distinguished Professorship in the Humanities at Valparaiso University.

Why Boredom Matters
Education, Leisure, and the Quest for a Meaningful Life

Kevin Hood Gary
Valparaiso University

CAMBRIDGE
UNIVERSITY PRESS

CAMBRIDGE
UNIVERSITY PRESS

University Printing House, Cambridge CB2 8BS, United Kingdom

One Liberty Plaza, 20th Floor, New York, NY 10006, USA

477 Williamstown Road, Port Melbourne, VIC 3207, Australia

314–321, 3rd Floor, Plot 3, Splendor Forum, Jasola District Centre, New Delhi – 110025, India

103 Penang Road, #05–06/07, Visioncrest Commercial, Singapore 238467

Cambridge University Press is part of the University of Cambridge.

It furthers the University's mission by disseminating knowledge in the pursuit of education, learning, and research at the highest international levels of excellence.

www.cambridge.org
Information on this title: www.cambridge.org/9781108839983
DOI: 10.1017/9781108878319

First published 2022

A catalogue record for this publication is available from the British Library.

ISBN 978-1-108-83998-3 Hardback
ISBN 978-1-108-81392-1 Paperback

*To my wife Heather and to our children Evelyn,
Lucas, and Gabriel*

CONTENTS

ACKNOWLEDGMENTS

First and foremost, I am grateful to my wife Heather for her constant love, support, and editorial gifts and for putting up and living with someone writing a book. Throughout the writing process, Heather offered invaluable direction, substantive feedback, and meticulous editing. Second, I am grateful to my dear friend Doug Yacek. Doug supported me during every phase of the writing process – carefully reading, editing, and providing feedback on multiple early drafts, providing needed encouragement and kindness throughout, and helping me to stay the course. Also, I owe a special debt of gratitude to my dear friend Mark Jonas who has, for the past decade, been a constant source of inspiration and scholarly support. At least in my case, I do not see how books can be written without a community of friends. With friends like Heather, Mark, and Doug, I am blessed beyond measure.

There are so many friends and colleagues I owe gratitude to. In particular, I am grateful to my dear friend Mark Hanafee for endless conversations about the meaning of life. I am grateful to my friends Dini Metro-Roland and John Fantuzzo, who carefully reviewed and offered substantive suggestions for multiple chapters. In addition, I am grateful to my dear colleague Mel Piehl who offered, from his vantage point as an intellectual historian, thoughtful and critical edits that improved the story I am trying to tell. In addition, I am grateful to my friends Tal Howard and David Weber, for their encouragement, feedback, humor, and friendship throughout this project. Also, I am particularly grateful to my friend Yoshi Nakazawa who encouraged me to further develop into a book an earlier chapter I wrote on boredom and contemplation. In addition, I owe a special debt of gratitude to my dear friend Alven Neiman, who directed my dissertation and lovingly pointed me in the direction of Kierkegaard, to grace, and to the wisdom of Abraham Heschel.

My family deserves a special mention. In particular, I am grateful to my daughter Evelyn whose artistic creations bear witness to the kind of leisure I hope to aspire to. I am grateful to my son Lucas whose sharp critique of school boredom inspired my writing. I am grateful to my son Gabriel who embodies a spirit of boundless leisure. I am especially grateful to my sister Megan, who is not only an expert psychiatrist but also a wise and loving friend. I am grateful to my mother and father, Patricia and John Gary (deceased in 2004), for their love and support of my educational endeavors. In addition, I am grateful to my mother's dear friend and partner Bob Johnson, for his generosity and kindness. Lastly, I need to express gratitude to my dear uncle John Kenny (aka. Johnny), whose love and practice of leisure inspired my own. And I would be remiss if I did not express gratitude to his amazing wife Luz Ramos, whose love radiates the grace that comes with the practice of genuine leisure.

Lastly, I owe a debt of gratitude to my home institutions, formerly Goshen College, Loyola Academy, and now Valparaiso University, for supporting my scholarship. Parts of the chapters in this book, at earlier stages, were conference papers. In addition, I was blessed to be the recipient of Valparaiso University's Baepler Professorship from 2016 to 2020, which provided valuable sabbatical time to begin work on this project.

INTRODUCTION

My interest in this book is with the problem of boredom, in particular how we are conditioned to both recognize and respond to it. Ultimately, I am interested in what is the optimal way to engage with this unpleasant and ubiquitous mood state. In spite of pedagogical "innovations," boredom is particularly acute in schools. Students overwhelmingly report being bored in school, especially in the higher grades (DePaoli et al., 2018). Given the extent of student boredom and its negative associations, including student misconduct (Lazarides and Buchholz, 2019), poor academic performance (Daniels et al., 2015), and dropping out of school (Bridgeland, 2010), this problem is particularly vexing for educators. In response, schools often do one or both of the following: First, endorse, perhaps unwittingly, what novelist Walker Percy (1916–1990) describes as a "boredom avoidance scheme" (1985, p. 11), adopting new initiative after new initiative in the hope that boredom can be outrun altogether. Second, they compel students to accept boring situations as an inevitable part of life, suggesting that maturity requires such compliance.[1] The combination of these two strategies, avoidance and

---

[1] Over the past 15 years, I have visited numerous K-12 classrooms, as part of a qualitative research project and also to observe students studying to become teachers. I am often struck by how boring and tedious the classroom spaces are. What is especially surprising to me, though, is how orderly and docile the students usually are. Instead of creating problems and/or finding ways to distract or amuse themselves (e.g., checking their phones or misbehaving) the students, most of the time, simply attend quietly to the low-level tasks at hand. On the surface, such student compliance might appear to be beneficial as students learn how to cope and endure

resignation, is arguably an ideal disposition for the modern worker, who needs a capacity to endure, without complaint, hours of tedious and mindless tasks, punctuated by weekends filled with consumptive diversions. This is not, however, ideal for human flourishing, either on an individual or communal level.

Resignation to boredom, or knee-jerk attempts to escape it, are similar in that both responses resist reflection on this problem. In a capitalist society, producers often want people to dread boredom and be unreflective about it, so consumption becomes simply a knee-jerk antidote to it. Given the pervasiveness of boredom, the multitude of negative behaviors that are causally linked to it, and the economic system that benefits from it, the problem of boredom merits careful attention, especially in education. When schools graduate students who are unable to endure boredom, and who cannot discern when to accept boredom or when and how to challenge it, then schools have failed to equip their students with an essential tool for navigating contemporary life.

Try as they might to outrun boredom, seeking to keep students engaged and/or entertained, most contemporary schools, in particular, cannot avoid it. Sterile architecture, bureaucratic management, perfunctory teaching to the test, and crowded spaces that silence unique expression contribute to this phenomenon. This hit home for me when my elder son started kindergarten. He had been looking forward to starting elementary school, and after his second day, I asked him how he liked it so far. He shared with exasperation, "I'm tired of hearing about hallway procedures." While schools do not explicitly teach about boredom, there is an implicit or latent curricular message conveyed to students and teachers alike: Boredom should be, first and foremost, avoided; if avoidance is not possible, then it should be endured as an inevitable, albeit unpleasant, part of life.[2] Aware of avoidance as a student's primary response, teachers are charged with appeasing and sustaining the fickle interests of their students. This places a heavy burden on teachers. Recognizing this

---

tedious situations. My concern, though, is how this coping is often marked by resignation – a dulling of the critical imagination. The students are conditioned to expect less, when they should expect more.

[2] This is part of the paradoxical nature of boredom – it pushes us to escape the present and/or prompts us to resign ourselves to a situation as hopelessly boring.

dynamic, students come to view boredom as primarily an external problem: If a classroom or other situation is experienced as boring, the environment must therefore be wanting in meaningful stimuli. School is boring, students are conditioned to believe, because of boring teachers, boring textbooks, and so on. This is both a missed opportunity and a miseducation.

Boredom, like anger, is a mood that will follow students beyond the walls of classrooms into workspaces; at family gatherings; into long lines at hospitals, grocery stores, and the DMV; at most jobs; in household chores; and in the grinding monotony that pervades nursing homes, where aging relatives and many of us will spend our final days. By ignoring the problem of boredom, we ignore a fundamental struggle with being human. When we are oblivious to how we deal with boredom, we fail to see how we are controlled by it – how we fashion lives that are essentially guided by boredom avoidance. Recognizing this problem, philosopher of education John Dewey (1859–1952) observed that if "education does not afford opportunity for wholesome recreation and train capacity for seeking and finding it, the suppressed instincts find all sorts of illicit outlets, sometimes overt, sometimes confined to indulgence of the imagination" (2018, p. 260). In short, the enduring problem of boredom needs attention.

In this book, I make a case that schools should graduate students who know how to engage boredom productively when it arises. Rather than simply avoiding boredom or helplessly blaming boredom on something or someone else, such students take responsibility for their boredom. They develop internal resources for contending with boredom; they are adept and diplomatic at challenging boring circumstances, and they are equipped at finding worthwhile activities and practices that alleviate boredom. Such students acquire a capacity to discern a creative middle way between boredom avoidance, on the one hand, and stultifying boredom endurance on the other.

This middle way, I will argue, is the practice of leisure. Boredom is not a new phenomenon. What is relatively new is the misguided assumption that we will find a technical and permanent solution to it. Given our constant digital innovations – which create seemingly endless possibilities for stimulation – it is not surprising that we hold out for a technological solution. This perspective, however, is mistaken. Boredom is not fundamentally a problem that can be addressed by adjusting environmental stimuli; rather, it is a problem that is rooted within the self. This is not to suggest that environment is negligible – some circumstances certainly prompt boredom more than others – but there is a leisurely versus bored way of relating with one's environment. The bored self, Søren Kierkegaard (1813–1855) reveals, is a self in despair. The tradition of leisure aims to address this despair. Instead of falling subconsciously into a cycle of boredom and boredom-avoidance, the leisure tradition offers an alternative way of being and engaging in with the world.

This book does not provide a new conception or psychological take on boredom. Rather, it considers this persistent problem in light of an enduring and viable solution: the practice of leisure. My argument proceeds as follows. In Chapter 1, I examine the moral significance of boredom and provide a brief overview of the history of American schooling vis-à-vis the problem of boredom and the practice of leisure. While the experience of boredom is rampant among students in K-12 education, thoughtful and direct engagement with boredom is largely absent in schools. This stands in sharp contrast with the vision for American secondary schools in the early twentieth century, which positioned the practice of leisure as an essential aim.

In Chapter 2, I explore the problem of boredom itself, drawing on recent research. In the last two decades, research interest on boredom has increased significantly across multiple disciplines. In particular, I focus on the enduring distinction Heidegger draws between situational and existential boredom. While Heidegger's diagnosis is insightful, the Heideggerian-inspired solution for existential boredom (the pursuit of authenticity) is deeply problematic.[3] What is needed, I argue, is a clearer moral framework to illuminate what is at stake when we are contending with boredom. Considering the phenomenon of boredom, Aldous Huxley notes a de-moralization of this phenomenon (1959). What

---

[3] I am finessing this point, as Heidegger's understanding of authenticity is far subtler and more nuanced than my critique suggests. My aim is not to take issue with Heidegger but with a version of this ideal that Charles Taylor rightly notes is pervasive in our time. On this point, see Chapter 2.

was previously regarded as a state of serious moral concern is now largely regarded as a neutral mood state, which may lead to good or bad outcomes.[4] This shift in perspective, I will argue, has both downplayed the problem boredom poses for human flourishing, and it undercuts our responsibility and complicity with this mood state. Suffering and avoiding boredom we are not simply losing interest in things; we are losing our moral compass. Boredom negatively impacts both our moral reasoning and our vision of human flourishing.

For clearer moral perspective on this issue, I turn to the writings of Kierkegaard in Chapter 3. Kierkegaard frames the problem of boredom as fundamentally a moral problem. Rather than offering a theoretical discourse about boredom, Kierkegaard creates a pseudonym or imagined-yet-familiar person (referred to as Poet A) who is afflicted with boredom and is seeking to outwit it. Poet A offers an in-depth look at the interior muddle that is the bored state. He also provides guidance for how best to cope with boredom, which, on the surface, sounds compelling, but is ultimately misguided. For insight on A's plight, we must look to Kierkegaard's more advanced pseudonym, Anti-Climacus, the author of *Sickness unto Death*. Anti-Climacus reveals that boredom is fundamentally a form of despair. To understand boredom, we must understand the self and the major kinds of despair the self is prone to experience.

In Chapter 4, I examine the ideal of leisure as a promising antidote to existential boredom. The practice of leisure, I argue, strikes a middle way between what Kierkegaard describes as the despair of possibility and the despair of necessity. Rather than a cycle of boredom and boredom avoidance, we can inhabit a leisurely way of being that permeates both engaging and "boring" activities. The practice of leisure, though, does not come easy. Leisure is best understood as an art that requires discipline, vigilance, and practice. In Chapter 5, I consider ways we can cultivate a leisurely state of mind, noting what kinds of practices, activities, forms of engagement, and rituals can help us learn and sustain the art of leisure.

---

[4] Huxley, of course, is referencing *acedia*, which is considered to be the ancient precursor of modern boredom.

In Chapter 6, I consider tangible ways we can educate for leisure, guiding students from a bored-avoidance way of being to a leisurely way of being. Finally, in the epilogue, I offer a coda on the pursuit of leisure. While schools (teachers and administrators) can make strides toward cultivating leisure in students, the art of leisure is fundamentally an individual task. It is learning how to be a person – how to live with and contend with the angels and demons that plague human existence.

1 THE MORALITY OF BOREDOM AND A BRIEF HISTORY OF LEISURE

Introduction

In the spate of scholarship on boredom over the past two decades, the moral character of boredom has received little attention (Elpidorou, 2017). This is striking because boredom's ancient precursor, acedia, was considered to be one of the deadliest vices and the source of several other destructive vices, including gluttony, lust, and anger (Bunge, 2011). In this respect, modern boredom arguably parallels acedia, as it is also casually linked to numerous problematic, arguably immoral, behaviors. The state of boredom is morally significant because it adversely impacts both moral reasoning and the vision of flourishing that guides moral reasoning. Boredom is not simply a mood we must endure but a state of mind (certainly impacted by circumstances) that we need not be captive to. Its moral significance also needs to be underscored because there is something at stake: We can do something about what we find to be boring (boredom assessment) and how we contend with this mood state (boredom endurance).

In this chapter, I first examine the moral significance of boredom and then consider how the US schools aimed to address the problem of boredom a century ago. Recognizing that students needed to be educated about how to spend their time well, the 1918 *Cardinal Principles on Secondary Education* report, published by the National Education Association's Commission on the Reorganization of Secondary Education, included leisure as an essential objective. More than just the cultivation of hobbies, the *Cardinal* report casts a vision of leisure as a guiding principle that animates all of life's activities; it clearly describes how leisure is necessary for human flourishing. I examine this report, its understanding of leisure, and then consider why this perspective has largely receded from the educational landscape. Rather than being seen as a public good, leisure is now largely deemed to be a private good – something the marketplace takes care of.

The Morality of Boredom

Half of the sins of humankind, Bertrand Russell wryly quipped, are because of our "fear of boredom" (1996, p. 36). Russell's observation holds up: Countless destructive behaviors are linked to boredom, including addiction (Biolcati et al., 2018), over-eating (Crockett et al., 2015), and gambling (Mercer and Eastwood, 2010). Yet, boredom avoidance also prompts subtler moral infractions, including half-listening – often as we check our phones – and frittering away time on trivial pursuits. We often think of morality in grand terms – sacrificing ourselves for others or standing up to a bully are two quintessential decision moments that make for good case studies in an ethics class. By contrast, responding well or poorly to boredom usually does not involve anything especially angelic or cowardly. On occasion, we hear about sensational and horrific crimes attributed to boredom, but most sins committed because of boredom fly under radar. Given the low moral stakes of most things that people do when they're bored, who are we to judge how others avoid boredom? And yet, I think most of us can see in our boredom avoidance tendencies ways of acting and spending time that fall short of what we might consider to be our better self. We might feel summoned or called to do great things but find ourselves busy avoiding boredom instead. Boredom, it turns out, is a productive topic for moral reflection. We deal with it regularly, making decisions each day to endure, avoid, or engage with boring situations.

It is hard to discern the optimal response to the problem of boredom because the symptoms are so varied and are often internalized. Einstein said that he pursued physics to "escape from everyday life with its painful crudity and hopeless dreariness, from the fetters" of his "ever-shifting desires" (2006, p. 225). Many turn to the media, news, or sports to alleviate boredom, or perhaps to reading books or pursuing hobbies. The development of a musical or athletic skill might be prompted and sustained by an escape from boredom. Yet, so too might the consumption of drugs be spurred by boredom avoidance. Crime, as noted, is also sometimes prompted by boredom. Such a curious range of activities and behaviors spring from boredom – from Nobel Prize–winning developments in physics to endless games of solitaire to random acts of cruelty. If Einstein had not discovered physics, might he have pursued other, less noble, boredom-evading pursuits? What is a right or healthy way to respond to boredom? We can certainly think of nonideal ways to respond to boredom, just as we can think of nonideal responses to anger or fear. Is it possible (or even desirable) to become unborable, as the travel writer David Fermor described himself? (2015, p. 25)

In spite of an endless stream of distractions served up on smartphones and other tech devices, the phenomenon of boredom persists. When I share with friends and acquaintances that I am writing a book on boredom, the response I almost always receive goes something like this: "Wow, that sounds really interesting." I am always struck that boredom, generally defined as a state of disinterest, is so interesting. I think this interest stems from our enduring desire to live well. Human beings desire to be happy, and boredom, clearly, is an obstacle to human flourishing. Even people who outwardly seem to be flourishing are afflicted with boredom. Given this, there is understandably an existential interest in this topic. It speaks directly to the self's desire for happiness. To understand boredom is to understand oneself – to begin to see how one's desires, hopes, and expectations assist with or impede an ability to flourish.

Boredom is sometimes referred to as a latent or hidden emotion, in contrast to anger or fear. As such, it is always lurking just beneath the surface, easy to overlook or ignore. We might consider ourselves to be largely immune from boredom, yet all the while caught within a boredom avoidance scheme. In this case, boredom may have more power than we realize. Whether consciously or not, we each have developed strategies to contend with boredom. We have also acquired ways of seeing and assessing what constitutes a boring situation. Again, while boredom feels objective (there is something that bores us), it is grounded in how we are conditioned to make sense of and engage with our environment.

This assessment varies from person to person and culture to culture. What feels like a natural and normal response is, in fact, a learned pattern of behavior.

The different cultural responses to boredom became especially apparent to me when I lived near an Amish community in northern Indiana. While shopping at the grocery store with my kids, I would frequently encounter Amish families doing the same. What for me was often a stressful experience – navigating the checkout line with three kids under the age of seven – seemed to be a stroll in the park for my Amish counterparts. Their children waited patiently, seemingly unmoved by the tantalizing display of candy, toys, and other items. Meanwhile, my kids could not resist the bait. Waiting in line is prime time for boredom to surface; the two sets of children had acquired different schema and habits for assessing, responding to, and coping with boredom.

The candy display at the checkout line is a small example, but it also underscores the moral significance of boredom. We are conditioned to avoid boredom through consumption of food, media, fashion, and so on. This is personally problematic because our bored state is often laced with despair of the self, whether it is about our image, our possessions, or lack thereof. Marketers, who are all too aware of this human foible, exploit it to their advantage. Landfills, chock full of old appliances, dated devices, and discarded home interiors provide evidence of our bored state run amok. The collective bored state of humanity fuels a level of needless and wanton consumption that our world cannot sustain.

The 2020 documentary *The Social Dilemma* illuminates how tech giants manipulate, direct, and hold our attention with algorithms that track and inspire our every move online (Orlowski, 2020). Social media feeds provide endless and personalized distraction, keeping us from ever having to confront our bored selves. While we are perhaps aware or suspect this is the case, this documentary features former Facebook and Twitter executives, and other tech mandarins, who pull back the curtain, revealing just how diabolically engineered and deliberate this process is. What is most striking (and not surprising) is how executives approach technology use with their own children. As one former Facebook leader noted, "We don't let our kids have really any screen time" (Orlowski, 2020).

To be sure, our society has changed how we deal with boredom. The most obvious change is in the means we have for keeping ourselves amused. All of these things (memes, YouTube, TikTok, Instagram, etc.) have certainly atrophied our attention span, causing what Adam Garfinkle describes as the erosion of deep literacy (2020). This cultural shift became clearer to me when reading Neil Postman's account of the Lincoln–Douglas debate in the 1850s (2005). On one occasion, Douglas spoke continuously for three hours. Following Douglas, Lincoln ascended to the podium, noted that the time was 5:00 PM, and said that he would need just as much time as Douglas to make his case, with Douglas then planning to make an hour-long rebuttal. Lincoln recommended that folks go home for dinner and return for his portion, which they did. Postman poignantly asks,

> What kind of audience was this? Who were these people who could so cheerfully accommodate themselves to seven hours of oratory? It should be noted, by the way, that Lincoln and Douglas were not presidential candidates; at the time of their encounter in Peoria they were not even candidates for the United States Senate. (2005, p. 44)

Postman goes on to ask, "Is there any audience of Americans today who could endure seven hours of talk? or five? or three?" The answer is an emphatic no – not in 1985 when Postman asked these questions, and certainly not in 2022 (p. 44). What accounts for this transformation? Certainly, our relationship with or intolerance for boredom is a key factor, as are the constant innovations to keep ourselves endlessly amused. Presumably, the Lincoln–Douglas debate attendees (or most of them) were not afflicted with boredom the way a modern audience would be? What kind of formation and development accounts for this difference?

Recent research on boredom is increasingly viewing boredom in a more positive light. While recognizing that it is an aversive, uncomfortable state, researchers are finding value in this curious mood state (Elpidorou, 2018; Gibbs, 2011; Mansikka, 2009; Scribner, 2019). Boredom, like other mood states, helps us navigate through our world. Philosopher Peter Toohey argues that boredom, as adaptive emotion, has evolved to help us "facilitate social relations by encouraging the beneficial rejection of toxic social situations" (2011, p. 33). Boredom is trying to tell or reveal something about ourselves and/or the environment. Philosopher Andreas Elpidorou makes a similar case, contending that boredom "should be understood to be a regulatory psychological state that has the capacity to promote our well-being by contributing to personal growth and to the construction (or reconstruction) of a meaningful life" (2018, p. 323). Yes, boredom can be a chronic and dangerous problem for those who suffer with trait boredom, but for most people, boredom is a transitory state – a form of pain that has something important to reveal to us, if we attend it. Elpidorou sums it like so: "boredom promotes movement; movement is essential to well-being; ergo, boredom promotes well-being" (2018, p. 323). The question, though, is movement toward what? What does well-being consist of? What constitutes a toxic social situation? Is this in the eye of the beholder? Children often find adult conversations to be dreary "social situations." Their assessment, though, is both true and not true. True, that the conversation bores them, but false, in that they often should attempt to understand and engage with the conversations they find themselves in.

In a recent and thoughtful appraisal of boredom, psychologists James Danckert and John Eastwood contend that though boredom "has a message for you, we would not be so bold as to tell you how to live your life" (2020, p. 2). "Boredom itself," they note, "can't tell you what to do, either. In that sense you are on your own. This is precisely one of boredom's key messages" (p. 2). What a strange mood it is then! Boredom is an evolutionary adaptive mood that tells us something, but we are not sure what it is telling us. Moreover, we are uncertain how best to alleviate the pain of boredom. And the apparent solutions to boredom, inspired by what medieval theologian Thomas Aquinas (1225–1274) describes as the "roaming unrest of the spirit," may only intensify boredom or prove to be short-lived (Pieper, 1990, p. 200).

This is largely where boredom research is at this point. Researchers continue to refine and sharpen our diagnosis of the problem but remain neutral on how best to contend with it. Boredom signals a misalignment of our desires with our environment, but with regard to the question of alignment, or how best to contend with boredom, we are on our own. This poses a serious challenge. First, our assessment of what is boring is often flawed and short-sighted.

Often what we initially find boring (e.g., a book and a new hobby), we later discover to be a source of great meaning and value. In this case, we may need to distrust rather than trust boredom. Rather than directing us to our well-being, boredom may blind us to sources of meaning and renewal that will benefit our well-being.

Second, boredom avoidance, as noted, can lead us down many questionable pathways. Yes, boredom prompts movement, but movement can take us in a thousand directions. It is the source of what Aquinas describes as *curiositas* (a voyeuristic kind of knowing) and the Buddhist tradition describes as monkey-mind – a restlessness that cannot sit still and is prone to needless chatter and busyness.[1] Third, boring circumstances are an inevitable part of life. Yes, ideally, we should hope for and pursue engaging and meaningful activities, but this expectation is often unrealistic and beyond our control. And conveying this message to students (that boredom is largely or exclusively an environmental problem) sets up a lens for boredom assessment that is largely driven by restless egotism.

Aiming for Leisure

We are not on our own in how we respond to boredom, nor should be at the mercy of opportunistic marketers. The struggle with boredom (while certainly more complex in our modern age) is an enduring problem that human beings have always wrestled with. That schools are dens of boredom and silent about its causes and cures is somewhat ironic given that the word school derives from the Greek word *skholē*, which means "leisure." While boredom is characterized as the inability or incapacity to enjoy time well, leisure is just the opposite. Leisure is the ability to cultivate pursuits that make life meaningful and an ability to redeem situations that appear barren of viable interests. While skholē, or an education for leisure, may sound like a distant ideal, as recently as 1918 *The Cardinal Principles of Secondary Education* (CPSE) report included leisure as one of seven essential aims for secondary students. This report served as a bellwether of national reform of secondary education in the United States. The leisure objective, it sets forth, merits quoting in full:

---

[1] On *curiositas*, see especially Paul Griffiths, 2006, pp. 47–63.

> Worthy Use of Leisure: The idea behind this principle is that education should give the student the skills to enrich his/her body, mind, spirit, and personality in his/her leisure. The school should also provide appropriate recreation. This principle should be taught in all subjects but primarily in music, art, literature, drama, social issues, and science. (Commission on the Reorganization of Secondary Education, 1918)

This objective took direct aim at the problem of boredom. In the early twentieth century, the "weekend" (or one to two days off from work) had just begun to take hold. People, especially in urban areas, were increasingly facing the challenge of what to do with free time. Recognizing the challenges inherent in knowing how to use leisure well, the CPSE report made this a top priority. That leisure was included in the report is noteworthy, but also significant is a view of leisure as a "principle" that "should be taught in all subjects." More than just time apart for the arts or hobbies, the CPSE called for a spirit of leisure to inform all the subjects. It is this conception of leisure, as a guiding principle, that I will explore in this book as an optimal response to the problem of boredom.

To operationalize the leisure objective schools, the CPSE called for the appointment of directors of leisure to oversee both the quality of instruction and extracurricular activities. More than mere education for work, or making a living, schools aimed to cultivate in students a way of living – an ability to spend time well – to discover ways to re-create the self. Schools sought to cultivate in students the capacity to recognize and savor the intrinsic worth of school subjects and activities, in addition to their extrinsic value. Directors of leisure were charged with ensuring that students were "developing interests that would assist them in later life to use their leisure wisely." While we tend to think of leisure as a matter of personal choice, without criteria, the CPSE noted good and bad uses of leisure. Pursuing the right kind of leisure, the CPSE explained that students will learn to re-create their "powers and enlarge and enrich life." Taking up the wrong kind of leisure, the CPSE goes on to note, "impairs health, disrupts home life, lessens vocational efficiency, and destroys civic-mindedness" (1918).

This 1918 CPSE report is the last instance when leisure was featured prominently in the taxonomy of educational objectives.

It has all but disappeared in the national educational discourse.[2] Today leisure is considered to be a private good. Given the high stakes economic sectors that profit from our leisure activities, it is perhaps not surprising that thoughtfulness about how we use our leisure time is absent from the curriculum. Moreover, apart from destructive forms of leisure (to oneself or others), how one spends their leisure time is largely regarded as a matter of personal discretion. In the 2010 Common Core Standards, the most recent articulation of national educational aims in the United States, leisure or anything approximating leisure, is completely absent. The verbs used in Common Core to describe what the mind is charged with doing include assess, critique, compare, analyze, evaluate, interpret, integrate, demonstrate, apply, and so on. Verbs we might associate with leisure (appreciate, wonder, enjoy, contemplate, admire, savor, and so forth) are conspicuously absent.

The Common Core is the latest iteration of national standards to voice what is deemed to be the most essential skills for the workplace. Spearheaded by the National Governors Association and the Council of Chief State School Officers, the Common Core standards were quickly adopted by forty states in 2010 and five more states over the next few years. The standards received widespread support from both political parties and the business community. Though there has since been pushback, with states pulling out of the Common Core, the subsequent standards created by individual states strongly resemble the Common Core standards. In short, this pragmatic, nonleisured vision reigns supreme.

The differences in the actual subjects referenced in the CPSE report of 1918 and the Common Core of 2010 is also striking. Not only is leisure absent from view, but the Common Core's exclusive focus on math, reading, and writing implies that other subjects, especially the arts, are nonessential and expendable. Common Core standards are part of a long history reflecting the philosophy of essentialism's dominance in the US education, which views the fundamental purpose of education as supporting economic and civic well-being. Our society needs certain skills and ways of thinking to

---

[2] The closest we come to stated anxiety about a loss of leisure is reflected in concerns about the limiting of recess and cutting arts. See, for example, https://time.com/4982061/recess-benefits-research-debate/.

compete in the world. The metaphor of education as a race that we need to win, and are at risk losing, is commonly invoked by political leaders across both parties. Essentialists believe we need to prepare for a future full of threats; hence, they focus on skills that will protect us from those threats.

Essentialism gained major traction after the Soviets launched the Sputnik satellite in 1957. Recognizing the American deficit in the space race, the Congress passed the National Defense Act in 1958. This was the largest federal educational initiative to date. The name of the act itself, the National Defense Act, conveys its view of education as necessary and vital to ensure a robust national defense. Students needed to learn essential skills, especially math and science, so the United States would remain competitive in the global and technological arms race. This vision of education was escalated with the Nation at Risk (NR) report, issued in 1983, which again sounded the alarm about schools again falling behind. The second paragraph of the NR report captures the tone and urgency of the situation

> If an unfriendly foreign power had attempted to impose on America the mediocre educational performance that exists today, we might well have viewed it as an act of war. As it stands, we have allowed this to happen to ourselves. We have even squandered the gains in student achievement made in the wake of the Sputnik challenge. Moreover, we have dismantled essential support systems which helped make those gains possible. We have, in effect, been committing an act of unthinking, unilateral educational disarmament (1983).

Applauding the strides made after Sputnik, thanks to the National Defense initiative, the NR report indicts our education carelessness, which had drifted from the essentials. Though the NR report was widely criticized for making specious claims (Berliner and Biddle, 1995), its effect was significant. The impact of this report leads directly to the No Child Left Behind initiative in 2001. Widely embraced by both major political parties, the No Child Left Behind ratcheted up testing in reading, math, and writing skills for American students. In order to continue receiving federal funding, states were forced to comply. School districts across the nation began a wave of testing to track the progress. Underperforming schools were quickly identified and penalized, and some were taken over or closed, which has made way for the charter school boom. The point of this brief history is to underscore how leisure has been completely displaced at an official level. In short, we do not have time for leisure or the problem of boredom, given our current educational arms race. The burdens of this hyper-pragmatic vision have invariably weighed down on poorer, more diverse schools, which have faced the most severe penalties for failing to meet testing benchmarks. No Child Left Behind benchmarks started in 2002 with a 50 percent passing rate as the requirement, which was raised up each year over ten years to reach a perfect 100 percent (Darling-Hammond, 2007). This draconian policy ensured that schools, especially in poorer communities, would fail to meet the passing rate and be publicly deemed as failing schools. Thus, while wealthier schools have time and resources to pursue nonessential subjects and activities where habits of leisure can take hold (preserving vestiges of the CPSE report's holistic vision), poorer schools have been especially saddled with the burden of teaching to the test.

While essentialism remains as the dominant vision in the US education, there are other narratives or visions at work in education. The biggest contender was progressivism, which was at its height at the time of the CPSE report in 1918. Progressivism, which traces a line from Jean-Jacques Rousseau to Friedrich Fröbel to Maria Montessori on up to John Dewey, espouses a more holistic vision of education. True education, according to progressivism, should develop the natural and unique potential of each child, rather than the interests of the state of the economy. Learning should begin with the natural interests of the child. Curriculum or the disciplines can appear as settled, well-organized fields of study. In fact, each discipline began with simple questions. A child's basic curiosity about plants, insects, or the stars are the nascent beginnings of a budding botanist, entomologist, or astronomer. Building on such interests, education can steer clear of boredom.

While the essentialist ignores the problem of boredom, the progressive narrative took direct aim at it. Considering traditional modes of instruction, Dewey asks how many students "came to associate the learning process with ennui and boredom?" A familiar question posed by students, especially in the later grades is, "Why do we have to do this?" or "What's the point?" This is often the question posed by the bored student. While perhaps off-putting, the fact that it is a question is evidence of a searching boredom that is trying to find some glimmer of meaning or purpose in the activity under question. The essentialist answers by saying, "You will need this skill or knowledge in the 'real world'" or when pressed the essentialist might say, "We are competing with China, and you need to learn this so we will remain competitive."

For progressives, questions like this, ideally, should not be an issue. Progressives aim to teach in such a way that questions about relevance or meaningfulness do not arise at all. While compelling, the progressive narrative risks playing into the unrealistic expectation that life should be endlessly stimulating – that our interests should be cultivated and satiated. Teachers, who are inspired by this vision, are motivated to make sure their content connects with, engages, and stimulates their students. This approach unwittingly endorses a boredom avoidance scheme, which hinders students from contending with the boredom they will inevitably confront.

To be sure, Dewey and his fellow progressives were all too familiar with this temptation or the mirage of appealing to unending interests. Dewey described this, literally, as the interests approach, where teachers appeal to and draw on student interest as the driving motive for learning (1913). Recognizing how fickle and short-lived interests can be, Dewey is critical, noting that in addition to interests, we need to prompt students to summon the will and put forth the effort to push ahead when interests wane, as they surely will. Sometimes, rather than avoiding boredom, we must learn to endure it. On other hand, Dewey cautions we cannot simply rely on student effort. Effort and interest must be balanced. This middle way is the space where the practice of leisure takes hold. This is the vision of leisure that the CPSE report upholds as the ideal. Tracing the tradition of leisure, which extends from Aristotle through St. Benedict up to the CPSE, I make a case for restoring leisure as a necessary, worthy, and vital aim for education today.

There are, however, two misconceptions vis-à-vis leisure that should be addressed at the outset. The first, and more recent misconception, is the association of leisure with vacation or other forms of amusement. I examine this further in Chapter 3. Leisure, according to this view, is simply free time set aside to do what we want. Given this understanding, leisure is a privilege for the elite, or those who have the means to partake of leisurely activities. This, though, is not the kind of leisure I am referring to. Leisure, rather than a respite or diversion from work, is a way of engaging with reality, a turn of the mind, that can permeate all activities. More than escaping from our weary or overworked self, leisure, in this sense, restores the self.

The leisure ideal draws from both ancient Greek and Hebraic sources. Where Greek leisure was a privilege for the few, Hebraic leisure was (and is) the right of the many, regardless of one's station. Where Greek leisure was tethered to a place (the Lyceum, the Academy, or the College), Hebraic leisure was instituted within and across time as a day of Sabbath rest. The class-based critique of leisure misunderstands the true nature of leisure itself. Genuine leisure transcends the classist privilege that associates leisure with wealth and status. More free time and money does not ensure genuine leisure.

The second and older misconception is the strong association of leisure with the liberal arts versus vocational arts. This perspective, which draws inspiration from Aristotle, tends to exclusively associate the practice of leisure with a form of ethereal knowing, pursued for its own sake. Leisure, according to this view, is also for a rarefied elite who have the resources and time to pursue nonutilitarian contemplative pursuits. While Aristotelian arguments like this can be justified, this view overlooks the more expansive vision and practice of leisure instituted by monastics like Benedict of Nursia (480–547). Also drawing from the Hebraic tradition of leisure, Benedict envisions and articulates a practice of leisure that animates both liberal tasks (contemplating the *Song of Songs* or Plato's *Timaeus*) and manual tasks (washing the dishes).[3]

It is this more comprehensive vision and practice of leisure that the CPSE report gestures to, criticizing a tradition of tying leisure

---

[3] All of the monastic brethren, Benedict insisted, regardless of their intellectual acumen, were required to do some work in the kitchen. See chapter 35 of the Rule "The brothers should serve one another. Consequently, no one will be excused from kitchen service" (516/1982, p. 57). To be sure, monks did not officially contemplate texts like Plato's *Timaeus*. Such texts were transcribed and preserved as embodiments of literary excellence (Leclercq, 1982). Nevertheless, Benedict's *Rule* calls for a spirit or principle of leisure animating every activity.

to an elite liberal education. As the CPSE committee member-at-large Henry Neumann explained, "The making of a living is to contribute to the making of a certain kind of life; and the vocational preparation is to keep this larger consideration in the forefront" (Wraga, 2001). Toward this end, the CPSE advanced a vision of the comprehensive high school as comprising both liberal and vocational options. Also, pushing against an overly utilitarian view of education, the CPSE report, as noted, posits a vision of leisure as a principle that should not only animate subjects like music and art but also subjects like math, history, and science.

In light of the problem of boredom, this book aims to restore leisure as a vital concern for schooling in the twenty-first century. When complaining about boredom, students are largely referring to situational boredom – a lack of meaningful stimuli in their environment. Presumably, the cure for such boredom simply involves simply modifying one's circumstance. Yet, the cure for situational boredom may only deepen existential boredom – a deeper restlessness about the meaning and purpose of life. Leisure is an alternative to the boredom avoidance scheme. Yet before making a case for leisure, I need to first examine further the problem of boredom – its underlying dynamics, and why it is so pervasive.

2 THE PROBLEM OF BOREDOM

"A generation that cannot endure boredom will be a generation of little people ... unduly divorced from the slow processes of nature, in whom every vital impulse withers, as though they were cut flowers in a vase." – Bertrand Russell (1930)

Introduction

To see how education can offer a space for contending with the ubiquitous problem of boredom, I first need to begin to define what boredom is and understand how it constitutes a "problem" for the pursuit of a flourishing life. The most vexing kind of boredom is what Heidegger describes as "existential boredom," characterized by a disenchantment with life and a struggle to find meaning. In contrast to situational boredom, which ebbs and flows depending upon external conditions, existential boredom is often an enduring condition that, while affected by material conditions, is not reducible to them. Situational boredom points to a clear and immediate solution in some kind of action, while the cure for existential boredom is often unclear. Even more problematic, as I will argue, the avoidance of situational boredom intensifies existential boredom. The pervasive cures for situational boredom are the cause of existential boredom.

The concept of situational boredom has been defined and extensively explored in field of psychology. My discussion of existential boredom draws especially on Heidegger's *The Fundamental*

Concepts of Metaphysics: World, Finitude, Solitude (1995).[1] Heidegger offers an intensive phenomenology of the experience of boredom, exploring the conditions that prompt situational or superficial boredom, as well as illuminating the deeper internal dynamics that undergird profound or existential boredom. Existential boredom, Heidegger contends, is the "fundamental attunement" or mood of the modern age (1995, p. 59). This condition, he contends, is grounded in the inauthenticity that pervades modern culture. Rather than forging an original existence, each of us is easily subsumed within the "They," mortgaging our unique self to the collective pressures of mass society. While ostensibly safe and comfortable, compared with other eras, such an existence is ultimately fraught with existential boredom. The presumed "cure," or answer for existential boredom, is to resist inauthentic assimilation and embrace the "ideal of authenticity" (1991, p. 16). Heidegger's existential ideal, as philosopher Charles Taylor notes (1931–), has become the reigning wisdom for human flourishing in a secular age. As enticing as this ideal is, however, I argue that this proposed remedy for existential boredom not only falls short but also marginalizes the bored self from traditional resources that might be of assistance in addressing the deeper roots of this condition.

The Emergence of Modern Boredom

The etymology of the word *boredom* is relatively recent. The words "bored," "to bore," and "boredom" first appeared in the late eighteenth and early nineteenth centuries, gaining significant traction in the twentieth century. Though boredom appears to be a modern concept, the phenomenon that it aims to diagnose has a long history that one can trace at least as far back to Qoheleth (the author of the biblical Book of *Ecclesiastes*, circa 935 BCE), if not further. Contemplating the paradoxes of life, Qoheleth renders the judgment that life is nonsense, or *hével* (the Hebrew word for vapor, translated as meaningless): "'Meaningless! Meaningless!' says the Teacher. 'Utterly meaningless! Everything is meaningless.'" To be sure, Qoheleth's meaninglessness sounds far more serious than

---

[1] This seminal and enduring work is based on a series of lectures Heidegger delivered in 1929.

situational boredom, but it does sound a lot like existential or profound boredom.

While Plato does not use a comparable term, his depiction of democratic youth in the *Republic* (no doubt a reflection of the youth of Athens in his day) resonates with this malaise, describing young people, especially in democratic societies, as often aimless, flitting from one thing to the next, taking on whatever catches their interest (375 BCE/1991).[2]

Evagrius, a Christian of the fourth century, recounts a similar phenomenon experienced by monks. Overcome by acedia (boredom's ancient precursor, which was also referred to as the noon-day devil), monks felt simultaneously weary and restless. Evagrius elaborates:

> The eye of the person afflicted with *acedia* stares at the doors continuously, and his intellect imagines people coming to visit. The door creaks and he jumps up; he hears a sound, and he leans out the window and does not leave it until he gets stiff from sitting.... [*Acedia*] makes it appear that the sun moves slowly or not at all, and that the day seems to be fifty hours long. Then he compels the monk to look constantly towards the windows, to jump out of the cell.... (Bunge, 2011, p. 28)

More than a mere malaise or sense of aimlessness, acedia was long considered one of the deadliest of sins, included among the eight deadly thoughts, which Gregory the Great later consolidated into the seven deadly sins. In Dante's *Inferno*, those who have committed the sin of acedia are placed in the fifth circle of hell. Dante describes their eternal fate within a mucky swamp: "Wedged in the

---

[2] The full quote from Socrates on the state of democratic youth reads as follows: "... he lives along day by day, gratifying the desire that occurs to him, at one time drinking and listening to the flute, at another time drinking water and reducing; now practicing gymnastics and again idling and neglecting everything; and sometimes spending his time as if he were occupied with philosophy. Often he engages in politics and, jumping up, says and does whatever chances to come to him; and if he ever admires any soldiers, he turns in that direction; and if it's money-makers, in that one. And there is neither order nor necessity in his life, but calling this life sweet, free, and blessed he follows it throughout" (Plato and Bloom, 1991, p. 240). This account resonates with how alleviating situational boredom may in fact exacerbate existential boredom.

slime, they say: 'We had been sullen in the sweet air that's gladdened by the sun; we bore the mist of sluggishness [*accidioso*] in us; now we are bitter in the blackened mud.'" (1995, p. 89). To give into acedia, then, was to despair in the face of the goodness of creation, the sweet air and the sun that Dante describes. Ultimately, though, acedia was considered despair vis-à-vis the grace of God.

With the advent of science and a materialistic worldview during the Enlightenment, the belief in acedia as a component of human sinfulness, and something to be alleviated by divine grace, largely faded. Human malaise was increasingly understood as reducible to physical rather than spiritual causes. While the exact nature of those causes remained speculative, there was supreme confidence that it would be understood and remedied. The term *melancholy* itself, appearing first in the fourteenth century, reveals this incipiently medicalized and materialized orientation. To suffer melancholy, it was believed, was to be afflicted with an excess of black bile – a substance thought to be secreted by the kidneys or spleen. The word melancholy comes from the Old French word *melancolie*, with *melan*, meaning black, and *chole*, meaning bile. While the black bile hypothesis was discarded by early modern investigators, the impulse to understand human malaise as reducible to physical causes, whether internal or external, endures.

The descriptor *boredom*, which took hold in the nineteenth century, is a middle or hybrid term between acedia, on the one hand, and melancholy, on the other. Boredom both reveals and connotes this complex lineage, while also being distinct from it.[3] Speculation about boredom's spiritual causality vis-à-vis God (as rooted in despair or sin) is largely absent in contemporary research. So too, while physical determinants are understood to play a part in the condition, contemporary boredom researchers are loath to entirely reduce boredom to material factors (whether internal or external). The search for the mysterious black bile is no more. Nevertheless, brain research continues to map correlations of the bored state with activity in various regions of the brain. This research is in its infancy, though, and of course it is made infinitely more complex given that boredom is part of human consciousness.

---

[3] For this understanding, I am indebted to Elizabeth Goodstein's masterful work *Experience Without Qualities* (2004).

While spiritual or material interpretations have been tempered, literary theorist Elizabeth Goodstein notes that they do persist as *a priori* frames for interpreting or making sense of the experience of boredom (2004). Empirical or materialist frameworks (prevalent in sociology, physiology, and psychology) attempt to trace the phenomenon, and its noted increase with modern life, "to the effects of modernization and urbanization on the human organism" (Goodstein, 2004, p. 12). Conversely, spiritually inclined interpretations (which endure in literary, philosophical, and poetic accounts) attempt to see something more significant at work. For such thinkers, boredom reflects deeper disturbances and has something meaningful to convey.

Both approaches, Goodstein contends, neglect the historical conditions that account for how this phenomenon has come to be understood. They fail to recognize how historical conditions, especially "the particular losses that plague modern life," inform verdicts about the "ultimate meaninglessness of existence" (Goodstein, p. 4). The experience of malaise, Goodstein contends, "cannot simply be abstracted from the language in which it is expressed, for what appears as immediacy is in fact construction. Each of these forms of discourse is embedded in an historically and culturally specific way of understanding and interpreting human experience," or what Goodstein describes as the *"rhetoric of reflection"* (Goodstein, p. 4). Boredom, according to Goodstein, is a historically situated phenomenon that is unique to modern life, given the loss of traditional meaning structures.

Qoheleth's vanity, Evagrius' acedia, and modern notion of boredom, Goodstein argues, each emerge from a particular historical and cultural context. They are distinct and relativized within a different medium. In any case, what is striking, though, are the similarities in the qualitative accounts of this phenomenon from Ecclesiastes (c. 450–200 BCE) to Evagrius (345–399) to Blaise Pascal (1623–1662) to Kierkegaard (1813–1855) to Sylvia Plath (1932–1963) to David Foster Wallace (1962–2008), as well as in recent psychological studies. While the larger metaphysical frameworks or assumptions have evolved (from spiritual to material ones), the two fundamental dimensions of this experience (restlessness and aimlessness) are consistently noted across time and culture. Industrialization, clock-time, and the conditions of modern life have certainly intensified and democratized boredom and given it a particular flavor, but the experience appears to be more universal than particular.

Philosopher Lars Svendsen shares Goodstein's historicist perspective, though he cannot resist enlisting a wide range of historical sources to illuminate this phenomenon, including Ecclesiastes. Yet turning to Ecclesiastes' poignant diagnosis of the meaninglessness of life, Svendsen claims that it is "not unreasonable … to say that Solomon [the tradition-ascribed author of Ecclesiastes] is here being prophetic rather than diagnostic on behalf of his age" (2008, p. 21). But completely historicizing the author in this way is itself unreasonable. It is more reasonable to contend that Solomon's words were diagnostic for his time and ours. Boredom is a perennial problem. It is not, as Svendsen contends, somehow the "'privilege' of modern man" (p. 21). Acknowledging this opens up the field of boredom studies to a wider range of diagnoses and possible remedies. There is, I will argue, wisdom to be gleaned about the phenomenon of boredom (its causes and possible cures) across the ages, from both classical and contemporary sources.

In one sense, the boredom problem seems simple and straightforward, as does the solution. We desire engagement and stimulation, and we recoil from situations that lack it. The goal then, presumably, is to maximize interest and minimize dullness. Thanks to modern technology, we continue to make strides at keeping ourselves distracted, continually devising more ingenious and multifarious ways to avoid boredom. Our smartphone usage rate proves this point. Teenagers spend on average 7 hours a day, or close to 50 hours per week, on their smartphones, with adults trailing close behind.[4] The Roman circus has advanced beyond our wildest imaginations: We are bombarded by omnipresent screens, with an endless supply of news, entertainment, and social updates. We are, as T. S. Eliot presciently observed, increasingly "distracted by distraction from distraction" (1971, p. 20). Yet, this situation is arguably more complex. Our smartphones serve multiple purposes. Many of the activities, for example, on phones, seem at least to have a wider valence – making social connections, keeping up with contemporary affairs and culture, etc. Our penchant for distraction

---

[4] https://abcnews.go.com/US/teens-spend-hours-screens-entertainment-day-report/story?id=66607555

is enmeshed within and often operates under a wide range of ostensible intentions or functions.

Of course, this trajectory of distraction raises several questions. First, why do we need to be endlessly amused? Why are we, as Pascal famously quipped, unable to sit still in a room without distraction? Simply put, why do we avoid boredom? We can certainly appreciate why enduring boredom is necessary at times (e.g., the sometimes tedious repetition required for mastering a new skill). But might there be other reasons why we should endure rather than resist it? Or, if we can reign in the obvious problems brought on by boredom avoidance (e.g., inefficient work and substance abuse), what is wrong with a life dedicated to steering clear of boredom as much as possible?

In the last two decades, research on the phenomenon of boredom has increased significantly. A recent EBSCO search from 1931 to 2000 yielded just 682 articles, while a search from 2001 to 2021 yielded 2,641 articles. This scholarship hails from multiple disciplines, including psychology, philosophy, literature, history, and education. This interdisciplinarity is not surprising given the complexity of this problem. The striking increase in boredom research also prompts the question, why has the question of boredom become so interesting to so many?

The varied, significant paths of this research may offer some clues. Primary lines of inquiry include "state versus trait" boredom (Hunter and Eastwood, 2018), the causes of boredom (Mercer and Eastwood, 2010), and diagnosis of the varieties or different kinds of boredom (Goetz et al., 2014). What are called state-versus-trait studies examine why some people are more prone to suffer boredom. Causality studies consider the degree to which boredom is an objective or subjective phenomenon, examining, for example, to what extent boredom is prompted by material conditions or person-dependent. Researchers also continue to nuance the phenomenon, noting different varieties or forms of boredom. Researcher Thomas Goetz and his team, for instance, have diagnosed five distinct types of boredom: indifferent, calibrating, reactant, searching, and apathetic (2013).

"Indifferent boredom" refers to a mild state of boredom – what we might experience sitting in the sun for an hour. We are not particularly stimulated, but we are also not particularly dissatisfied. "Calibrating boredom" refers to a budding disinterest with what we are supposed to be engaged with. Kierkegaard describes the experience of a student being trapped listening to a professor drone on endlessly. Overcome by boredom, the student's mind begins to wander until he notices beads of sweat streaming down the professor's face, forming into droplets that hang precariously from the professor's nose. The calibrating mind is searching for something, anything, to stimulate its attention. "Reactant boredom," like calibrating boredom, is also restless, but more volatile. Suffering "reactant boredom" describes a condition where we literally cannot sit still. "Searching boredom" pertains to the larger quest to find hobbies or work that will keep us meaningfully engaged.

"Apathetic boredom" refers to a much bleaker state of boredom. While reasonably content in a state of indifferent boredom, or inclined (or driven) to overcome calibrating, reactant, or searching boredom, apathetic boredom is characterized by a state of resignation and a sense of helplessness. When we experience apathetic boredom, we are stuck in a bored situation without end. We are bored with our life at large, and we are unable to see a way out.

And yet another kind of boredom researchers have diagnosed maps on to what Scottish novelist Robert Louis Stevenson describes as the "weariness of satiety" or boredom prompted by over-stimulation (1880). This sounds counterintuitive, given that boredom is usually linked to under-stimulation. In the case of a "weariness of satiety," an oversaturation of stimuli hinders the ability to attend to any one thing (Eastwood et al., 2012).

While nuancing the varieties of boredom is valuable work, as these psychological studies do, the focus here is on the primary distinction between situational and existential boredom that Heidegger diagnoses. Moreover, Goetz's typology readily fits within Heidegger's larger frames, with indifferent, calibrating, reactant, and searching boredom being a subspecies of situational boredom and apathetic boredom being interchangeable with existential boredom. For many scholars, the situational–existential distinction remains the most salient one (Svendsen, 2008; Toohey, 2011), and it is the primary set of paired conditions dialectically addressed here.

Situational Boredom

The preponderance of boredom research focuses on situational boredom rather than existential boredom. This is not surprising given that situational boredom is easier to diagnose and quantify. It can be replicated within a laboratory setting, with researchers subjecting a group of subjects to a boring task (e.g., copying names out of a phone book), alongside a control group. Observable behaviors can then be carefully documented, followed by eliciting qualitative feedback. Researchers can then code for themes across a statistically significant sample size. This work generates valuable insight into the dynamics of situational boredom, noting its causes and consequences.

To be situationally bored, note psychologists Danckert and Eastwood, is to be "painfully stuck in the here and now, bereft of any capacity for self-determination, yet driven to find something that we can engage with" (2020, p. 19).[5] Three key conditions stand out for those suffering situational boredom. The first is simple under-stimulation. Boring situations that lack stimulation (whether real or perceived) are irritating to varying degrees, depending upon their nature and duration. The mind seeks to be engaged, and boring environments lack meaningful or interesting possibilities for engagement. Under-stimulation is actually painful to those undergoing it. This insight was sensationally illustrated by the shock test conducted at the University of Virginia in 2014 (Wilson et al., 2014). Participants were asked to sit with their thoughts for 15 minutes, or they could opt to push a button and self-administer a painful shock. The results were (pun intended) shocking: 67 percent of men and 25 percent of women chose to shock and hurt themselves rather than endure even a brief span of time free of stimulation.[6] Also interesting is the striking gender imbalance. Women, this study suggests, are better at coping with under-stimulated situational boredom than men.

Boring situations seemingly offer little or nothing with which to engage. Heidegger shares the example of sitting at a remote train station (before smartphones existed), having to wait hours before his train departs. The station itself offers nothing of interest, and he is left wanting for something to pass the time. Such situational boredom, notes Heidegger, is "not simply an inner spiritual experience";

---

[5] A key and complicated distinction is between boredom and boredom avoidance. This is difficult to disentangle. In avoiding boredom, we are still bored and often persist with being bored.

[6] Timothy D. Wilson et al. (2014). Just think: The challenges of the disengaged mind. *Science*, 345(6192), 75–77.

there is *something* that bores us – even if it is an absence (1995, p. 83). The boring thing or situation "does not stimulate and excite, it does not give anything, has nothing to say to us, does not concern us in any way" (1995, p. 84). Stuck at the station, Heidegger literally feels the time moving slowly. His experience of the extension of time under such conditions correlates with the German word for boredom, *Langeweile*, which literally means "long while." Heidegger's assessment is not simply a cognitive inventory of limited options for mental engagement, but rather a felt sense of impoverishment. A bored person *feels* the barrenness of her situation. It leaves her groping for something, anything, to occupy herself with. One can imagine Heidegger considering a number of options with which to pass the time. He is, though, simultaneously caught in an *akratic* or weak-willed state, unable to wrest his way out of it. He describes it this way: "That which bores, which is boring, is that which holds us in limbo and yet leaves us empty" (1995, p. 87). The being held "in limbo" is the feeling of vacant time passing slowly, with nowhere to turn to alleviate the boredom that oppresses. The "leaving us empty" is our indifference to the situation and what it presents. There is nothing there that piques and holds Heidegger's interest (p. 87).

The second key condition in situational boredom is the loss of agency. To suffer boredom is to find one's environment wanting in meaningful stimuli that activate the self. The familiar complaint from children, "I'm bored; there's nothing to do," captures this sentiment. The judgment about "nothing to do" indicates a situation that is seemingly barren of interest (an objective condition) but also reveals how the imagination is diminished (a subjective condition). Overcome by boredom, those in such circumstances, literally cannot see or imagine something worthwhile to do. Faced with limited options for engagement, boredom curtails agency both objectively and subjectively. Harry Frankfurt states:

> Being bored involves a radical reduction in the sharpness and steadiness of attention. The level of our mental energy and activity diminishes. Our responsiveness to ordinary stimuli flattens out and shrinks. Within the scope of our awareness, differences are not noticed and distinctions are not made. Thus, our conscious field becomes more and more homogeneous. As the boredom expands and becomes

increasingly dominant, it entails a progressive diminu-
tion of significant differentiation within consciousness.
(2004, p. 54)

Viable agency entails a capacity to imagine possibilities for meaningful engagement, coupled with the willpower to execute one of
them. Boredom both challenges our imaginative faculties by leaving
them nothing to act upon and enervates the will. Nothing stimulating comes to mind, or the possibilities that do come to mind seem
unappealing. They do not attract and move the will. What might
alleviate boredom (a walk, reading a book, a new documentary) has
lost its luster and thereby loses its motivational force. This perhaps
explains why the shock option was so appealing to so many participants. Painful, as it is, it is nevertheless an exercise of agency. It is
a choice, albeit a bleak one.

Given the pain of under-stimulation and the restriction of
agency, the third condition of situational boredom, restlessness, is
to be expected. Boredom, notes Elpidorou, pushes or propels us to
engage with something, anything, different (2020). When suffering
boredom, we often literally cannot sit still. This dimension of situational boredom is especially poignant in former prisoner Jim Quillen's account of the nineteen days he spent in solitary confinement
at Alcatraz Penitentiary (1991). In total, Quillen served time in
Alcatraz for 10 years, from 1942 to 1952. The D Block at Alcatraz
consisted of forty-two confinement cells. Each cell was 9 × 14 ft,
included a small toilet, and was completely walled in except for
a steel door that blocks out all light once it is closed. Inmates in
solitary confinement were confined to total darkness for 24 hours a
day, "except when a slot in the door [was] opened briefly to allow
a meal to be slid inside" (2016, p. 202). Quillen recounts the following story of how he used to pass the time: "What I used to do is
I'd tear a button off my coveralls, flip it up in the air, then I'd turn
around in circles, and I'd get down on my hands and knees and I'd
hunt for that button. When I found the button, I'd stand up and I'd
do it again" (p. 202). This bleak account underscores how the mind
craves stimulation and will seek all manner of recourse, no matter
how trivial or unproductive, to secure some form of engagement.

Exposed to stark situational boredom and the agitation and
discomfort it brings, we are prompted to do something, anything to

escape. Rather than maintain a posture of thoughtful discernment, when we feel bored, we are pressed to find an immediate solution. Our agency is not only imaginatively reduced but also conscripted to take prompt action. Boredom both narrows the range of promising possibilities to pursue and pushes us to act. Facing this predicament, the easy alternatives, or quick and fast ways of distracting ourselves, come to mind most readily. It is not surprising that the bored state (painful, cramped, and restless) is associated with so many problematic behaviors (loss of attention, substance abuse, risk-taking, to name just a few). Our judgment is often impaired when we are afflicted by boredom and seeking an immediate resolution.

In light of the psychological features of situational boredom (under-stimulation, restricted agency, and restlessness), we can better see how we might steer clear of it. We need to maintain a steady diet of stimulation, along with preserving a free range of options, so our agency remains intact. Boredom, however, is a tricky foe. Recall how boredom can also be prompted by too much stimuli – the "weariness of satiety" Stevenson describes. In the case of this kind of boredom, the first two conditions of situational boredom (under-stimulation or compromised agency) do not apply. We may have, literally at our fingertips, an endless array of possibilities and yet still be bored.

To complicate matters, we may find ways to amuse ourselves, keeping situational boredom at bay, only to realize later that we have spent our time *choosing to do* what we neither really wanted nor desired. Leo Tolstoy's protagonist Alexei Vronsky in *War and Peace* illuminates this predicament:

> In spite of the complete fulfilment of what [Alexei] had so long desired, he was not completely happy. He soon felt that the realization of his longing gave him only one grain of the mountain of bliss he had anticipated. That realization showed him the eternal error men make by imagining that happiness consists in the gratification of their wishes. When first he united his life with [Anna's] and donned civilian clothes, he felt the delight of freedom in general, such as he had not before known, and also the freedom of love—he was contented then, but not for long. Soon he felt rising in his soul a desire for desires—boredom. Involuntarily he began to snatch at every passing caprice, mistaking it for a desire and a purpose. (2021, p. 548)

The case of Alexei suggests a kind of boredom that is not entirely or primarily situational. He is able, as Tolstoy notes, to satisfy his whims, but his fulfillment is short-lived. More than objective conditions (or the trappings of situational boredom), Alexei is contending with a subjective longing – what Tolstoy describes as a "desire for desires." All the more striking is Tolstoy's description of Alexei's response: an involuntary snatching "at every passing caprice." This case confounds a diagnosis of standard situational boredom. Indeed, Tolstoy's Alexei stands on the threshold of existential boredom.

Existential Boredom

While situational boredom is characteristically linked to an objective condition, existential boredom is harder to diagnose. Our situation may abound with stimulating possibilities, and yet we may suffer with existential boredom. In the case of situational boredom, Heidegger explains, we are bored "with something." There is a "determinate boring thing" or situation (1995, p. 119). For existential boredom, the cause is indeterminate. Existential boredom is not a particular situation or occasion that bores us, but rather a mood that casts a cloud over the whole of life. The novelist James Joyce (1882–1941) captures this pallor, describing his native Dublin, and its "brown brick houses," as "the very incarnation of Irish paralysis" (1944, p. 210). Moods (boredom, anxiety, euphoria) shape how we see and experience the world. While situational boredom is a passing state or emotion, conditioned by objective factors, existential boredom is a persistent mood, the source of which is uncertain. To be clear, moods are not merely subjective states. They are in-between states that reveal something about the world and the subject (Svendsen, 2008). Joyce's pithy observation reveals something about Dublin as well as about the state of his soul.

Given its peculiar subjectivity, the most perceptive accounts of existential boredom are often to be found in literary sources, whether fictional or autobiographical. In The Bell Jar, Sylvia Plath's protagonist Esther Greenwood offers an especially clear diagnosis. Weary with life, Esther is wondering why she should persist with basic tasks. "It seemed silly," Esther reflects, "to wash one day when I would only have to wash again the next. It made me tired just to think of it. I wanted to do everything once and for all and be done with it." Looking ahead at the trajectory of her life, Esther sees only a monotonous repetition:

> I saw the days of the year stretching ahead like a series of bright, white boxes, and separating one box from another was sleep, like a black shade. Only for me, the long perspective of shades that set off one box from the next day had suddenly snapped up, and I could see day after day after day glaring ahead of me like a white, broad, infinitely desolate avenue. (1979, p. 105)

Echoing Tolstoy's Alexei, Esther is unsure of what is even *worth desiring*. Her self-diagnosis, while sharper, is also starker. While Alexei, as Tolstoy notes, continues to grasp for something, Esther, seeing through the vanity of everything like Ecclesiastes' Qoheleth, questions whether there is anything worth striving for. She has not only lost the will or desire to do anything, but also a "desire for desires."

To be mired in existential boredom is to be lost or caught in a fog. Alexei's snatching at every "passing caprice, mistaking it for a desire and a purpose," illuminates how blinding it can be, and how blind we often are at diagnosing it. With existential boredom, there is an unsettledness or aimless restlessness that is difficult to gain perspective on, especially when we are in the throes of it. Given its opacity, understanding it requires intensive self-reflection and insightful guides. Suffering existential boredom, we are often like Dante, "lost in a dark wood," and, similar to Dante, we need a Virgil (or poetic guide) to illuminate our condition and hopefully point to a way out.

At this point, it is appropriate to distinguish existential boredom from depression. While they share many of the same characteristics, they are distinctly different mood states. "Depression," note psychologists Danckert and Eastwood, "is defined by sadness and an inability to feel pleasure" (2020). Depression includes negative self-appraisal and tendency to fixate on negative events. Boredom, by contrast, is "defined by the conundrum of wanting to be engaged but being unable to satisfy that want, a feeling that time is dragging on, and a difficulty in concentrating." The relationship between depression and boredom (which causes which) remains uncertain (Spaeth et al., 2015). Recalling Plath's Esther, she might be better described as being more depressed than bored. The key distinction between the two states pertains to hope. With the bored state, there is an underlying sense of hope, though it is often passive, that something in the future might be engaging and meaningful (Bargdill, 2019). With the depressed state, this sense of hope is absent – it sees or expects nothing of interest on the horizon.

Boredom is a peculiar mood. Where the mood of anxiety or euphoria heightens or intensifies our interest in the world of things, existential boredom removes or detaches all interest in the world of things. Afflicted with existential boredom, the world of things and stimulation loses its appeal. To experience existential boredom, in extreme, is to feel radically alienated from everything. Boredom, Heidegger explains, "like a muffling fog, removes all things and human beings and oneself along with them into a remarkable indifference" (1995, p. 12). When existential boredom becomes profound, this mood becomes totalizing; it colors all we see or, rather, *dis*colors everything, turning everything into a listless gray. Plagued with profound boredom, we no longer say "I do not know" (Stutz, 2017, p. 135). Profoundly bored people cease to "raise questions about themselves and about the world in which they live ... they have foreclosed on the possibility of fresh knowledge, assuming instead a position of false cognitive clarity" (Stutz, 2017, p. 136).

What is also striking is the subtle arrogance that accompanies the bored state. The bored self has rendered a dismissive judgment about the world and its possibilities. Rather than a posture of attention to something new, the bored self withholds

> full attention from an object, boredom in effect dismisses this object to the margins of one's prescription or interest. But this dismissal is, oddly enough, also a kind of closure, for to claim that something is boring is to claim that one knows something about an object. It is in fact to claim that one knows everything one needs to know about it in order to judge its relative worth. Like complacency, boredom is a totalizing move that excludes the potential for further questioning. (Stutz, 2017, p. 136)

Stutz's analysis suggests that a purely analytical treatment of boredom is inadequate and that some kind of moral appraisal is also called for. Boredom is not simply a psychological state that comes upon us as passive recipients but is a volitional, "totalizing move" – a form of *incurvatus in se* or the self pridefully turning inward and dismissing outward possibilities.

Attempting to illuminate this phenomenon further, Heidegger shares the story of going to a dinner party with friends. It is a pleasant evening, with the time passing by without notice. At the end of the night, however, he realizes after the fact how boring the whole affair was. He is perplexed by this because during the dinner, he did not experience the pain, restricted agency, and restlessness associated with situational boredom. At no point during the dinner did he recognize an itch to pass the time – a signature feature of situational boredom. Instead, he was content, or so he thought. It was not until afterward that he discovered how bored he truly was – and how pointless and dull the discussion was.

This leads to a crucial feature of existential boredom, and one that both complicates any direct attempt to grapple with it and yet it simultaneously points a way out. What is striking about Heidegger's account (and Plath's account of Esther) is that it includes what we might call an epiphany or revelation, whereby he "realized" the evening was boring. This revelation might not have come. We could just as easily imagine Heidegger or his friends not having such an epiphany and looking forward to more dinner parties to come. This awareness, though, did emerge. It might have been fleeting, with Heidegger resuming his normal course of life, or it might inspire him to radically change the way he interacts with his friends, or to find new friends altogether.

This raises an important question: If Heidegger had not experienced this revelation, would he still be existentially bored? Heidegger answers in the affirmative. While previously unrecognized, he now sees how this mood had existed as an unrecognized force, guiding and informing his actions. He sees dinner parties as part of a larger boredom avoidance scheme. He discovers that his success at staving off situational boredom unwittingly intensified his existential boredom. Like Esther, and, to a certain extent, Tolstoy's Alexei, what becomes clear to Heidegger is an awareness or nagging sense that his life, writ large, is boring and pointless.

The question that lingers with Heidegger's account is causal. What is at the root of his existential boredom? Why does it persist, and how can it be alleviated? As noted, existential boredom does not have the obvious objective referent in the way that situational boredom does. More problematically, it may not even be a conscious state of mind. Are we then, with respect to discerning existential boredom, at the mercy of the fortuitous epiphanies that Heidegger and Esther experience, while Alexei does not?

Reflecting on the omnipresence of the same phenomenon Heidegger identifies, boredom avoidance, author-essayist David Foster Wallace speculates on the deeper forces at work. Something, Wallace wonders,

> must lie behind not just Muzak in dull or tedious places any more but now also actual TV in waiting rooms, supermarkets' checkouts, airport gates, SUVs' backseats. Walkman, iPods, BlackBerries, cell phones that attach to your head. This terror of silence with nothing diverting to do. I can't think anyone really believes that today's so-called "information society" is just about information. Everyone knows it's about something else, way down. (2011, p. 93)

What is this "something else, way down" to which Wallace is referring? More than a snapshot of modern life, or a description of the way things have evolved with modern technology and our desire for constant stimulation, Wallace suggests that existential boredom points to a deeper rift within the self. While existential boredom is a mood that can exist within the psyche of a single individual, it plays out on a macro-level, evident in a culture that is rife with constant noise and distraction. It is not accidental that the news media has evolved into an endless stream of "breaking" stories and "crises," each one superseded by something more urgent. Everything, notes Kierkegaard, "even the most insignificant project, even the most empty communication, is designed merely to jolt the senses or to stir up the masses, the crowd, the public, noise!" (2015, pp. 47–48). We are indoctrinated into this boredom avoidance scheme. Avoiding existential boredom, Kierkegaard observes,

> We become sleepless in order to invent ever new instruments to increase noise, to spread noise and insignificance with the greatest possible haste and on the greatest possible scale … communication is indeed soon brought to its lowest point

with regard to meaning, and simultaneously the means of communication are indeed brought to their highest with regard to speedy and overall circulation. (2015, pp. 47–48)

Written in 1843, Kierkegaard's account of certain features of advanced modernity is diagnostic but also prophetic. While material conditions (work and amusement) continue to evolve, the human penchant and increasing demand for distraction endures.

This brings us yet closer to the source of the underlying condition. Drawing on Kierkegaard, Heidegger sees existential boredom avoidance as pervasive and amplified by modern conditions. "Each and every one of us," Heidegger says, "are servants of slogans, adherents to a program, but none is the custodian of the inner greatness of *Dasein* [German for 'being there'] ..." and its authentic possibilities for being in the world (1995, p. 163). In allowing ourselves to confront boredom, rather than run from it, letting it hit us with full force, and resisting the urge to escape, Heidegger sees a way to prevail over the fundamental condition of existential boredom, and thereby resisting the trap of chronic boredom avoidance. Facing directly what Heidegger describes as a "moment of vision," terrifying as it is in its seeming emptiness, we can see through clearly our tendency to let "life pass by as a series of inauthentic diversions" (1995, p. 172). We are then able to see ourselves and our culture as shot through with inauthenticity.

This is, in essence, Heidegger's answer to the question that Wallace posed earlier. The "something else, way down" that begets existential boredom is our incapacity to see and enact our lives as authentic expressions of our individuality. Heidegger is hopeful that once we allow ourselves to reach the nadir of boredom, a vision of possibilities for authentic existence will come into view. The way out, it turns out, is to go through. "When hit by boredom, let yourself be crushed by it; submerge, hit bottom" (Brodsky, 1995). Wallace's protagonist in *The Pale King,* an IRS accountant mired within the bowels of its tedious bureaucracy, reaches this state of paradoxically generated nirvana:

> The underlying bureaucratic key is the ability to deal with boredom.... To breathe, so to speak, without air. The key is the ability, whether innate or conditioned, to find the other side of the rote, the picayune, the meaningless, the

repetitive, the pointlessly complex. To be, in a word, unborable.... If you are immune to boredom, there is literally nothing you cannot accomplish. (2011, p. 390)

This is a movement toward a higher degree of freedom in contrast to "involuntary snatching" that permeates chronic boredom avoidance. Like Plato's freed prisoner in the Allegory of the Cave, we are able thereby to see through the facade that has kept us enthralled and submerged in the inauthenticity of the crowd.

Heidegger's (1927/1962) reflections on boredom provide the groundwork for his later magnum opus, *Being and Time*. There he notes how Being "has, in the first instance, fallen away from itself as an authentic potentiality for Being it-Self, and has fallen into the world" (*Being and Time* 38: 220). This state of fallenness is characterized by being "sunk in everydayness," most evident, Heidegger notes, in our proneness for idle talk, curiosity, and ambiguity (*Being and Time* 38: 220). Idle talk refers to chatter that stagnates and fails to open new possibilities for being. By curiosity, Heidegger is referring to the itch for constant stimulation and novelty. Entire industries are built on this proclivity. Ambiguity is the result of being taken in by the first two. It refers to "a loss of any sensitivity to the distinction between genuine understanding and superficial chatter" (Wheeler, 2020). Prone to staying on the surface, we are subsumed into the "They."

The Quest for Authenticity

Heidegger posits the meaning-making authentic self as the phoenix that can potentially rise from the ashes of existential aimlessness. This solution, and its companion ideal of individual authenticity, has gained cultural traction. It has become, as philosopher Charles Taylor notes, arguably the most compelling ideal of our time.[7] While Heidegger articulates a fuller vision of this ideal, the roots certainly trace back to the Romantic era and within the American context to the thought of Ralph Waldo Emerson. The mantra, "To thine own self be true" has become part of our social imaginary. While

---

[7] On the history of this ideal, see especially Taylor's chapter 13, "The Age of Authenticity," (2007, pp. 473–504).

often dismissed as narcissistic or hedonistic, as Allan Bloom does in his *The Closing of the American Mind* (Bloom and Bellow, 1987), Taylor discerns a nobler aspiration at work in this insistence on individual self-fashioning – a quest for happiness that is singular and unique. Human flourishing, according to the doctrine of authenticity, involves recognizing "that each of us has an original way of being human."[8] There is a unique way of "being human that is my way. I am called to live my life in this way, and not in imitation of anyone else's." In our flight from existential boredom, often subconsciously pursued, we forgo the summons to authenticity. The path into authenticity therefore involves embracing, not running from, existential boredom. This difficult step must be made with eyes wide open, which, in turn, enables us to recognize the inauthentic practices that mire us down rather than free us.

Assuming that we can emerge from utter meaninglessness, and discover wellsprings for authentic action, the ideal of authenticity, nevertheless, places a heavy burden on the subject. Given how interconnected we are with the culture in which we live, it is doubtful whether we can arrive at or achieve a pure authentic self, unaffected by the influence of those around us. Moreover, the ideal of authenticity, which seemingly opens up endless possibilities, also forecloses several options. We are compelled to move forward on a difficult personal quest, tasked with fashioning an original self. Given this trajectory, traditions and exemplars from the past, which propose and embody substantive ways of being and flourishing, are jettisoned as imitative and therefore inauthentic. The *authentikos* (Greek for genuine) is charged with moving ahead, starting anew, unbounded by tradition.

From the standpoint of moral or social criticism, the ideal of authenticity both narrows and expands the range of human responsibility. On the one hand, we are not responsible for the fallen state of inauthenticity we find ourselves in; on the other hand, we are charged with the extraordinary responsibility of fashioning a true self entirely on our own, without the resources we might cull from traditional sources. Society is corrupt and inauthentic, while the single individual – if courageous and insightful enough – is potentially

---

[8] On Taylor's response to Bloom's critique, see especially pp. 13–16 (Taylor, 1991).

pure and authentic. Resisting pressures to conform or to imitate others, the person striving for authenticity is attempting to respond to the summons to be true to themselves. Authenticity is a call to exercise one's personal agency in a robust way.

This account, on a certain level, rings true. For example, the decision about one's profession or life partner (assuming such choices are available) ought to be informed by a discernment process that aims to be faithful to one's deepest desires, rather than governed by social pressures. Yet, attempting directly to face down all assaults of existential boredom so as to see with the clarity how our life is shot through with inauthenticity is a precarious endeavor. The terror that is solitary confinement suggests this, as do many literary accounts of protagonists who see with piercing clarity their state of existential boredom.

Two of Fyodor Dostoevsky's characters, Ivan in *The Brothers Karamazov* and the unnamed protagonist in his short story "The Dream of a Ridiculous Man," offer lucid insight into existential boredom – their own and their culture at large. Yet rather than becoming a wellspring that motivates them to authentic expression, this discovery of the absurd meaninglessness of life prompts each of them to seriously contemplate suicide, which perhaps can be viewed as a grim expression of authenticity.

So, too, Plath's Esther, with a clear vision of the vanity of everything, contemplates and attempts suicide multiple times. Given how treacherous hyper-conscious awareness of existential boredom can be, is it arguably better to be inauthentically engaged with diversions than take on such risks on the path toward authenticity. Is it preferable to remain superficially engaged with shallow pursuits or morbidly disinterested in all of life's multiple enterprises and opportunities?

While the authenticity ideal's aspiration to practice a more vigorous agency is laudable, several questions arise. First, does it place too great a burden on the individual to stand apart from the social context they are immersed in? Second, and a related point, does authenticity, which prompts us to turn inward for enlightenment, risk eclipsing sources beyond the self that may provide resources for becoming a better self? Finally, is this ideal at risk for exploitation? Recognizing the existential need for authentic self-expression, the marketeers of capitalism are adept at inundating us with novelties that are pitched as seemingly indispensable means or accessories for becoming our true, authentic self. Walker Percy observes with amusement this dynamic in the common reply from a salesperson when we try a new shirt on: "It's you." This response appeals to the pursuit of authenticity, suggesting that our true identity, or our authentic identity, is amplified and fulfilled by our purchases. And yet, over time, the authenticity-imparting value of each purchase wears out, as the trends morph from season to season. Also ironic is the perception that we can fashion an authentic self by buying products that millions of others are also buying.

Of course, we can engage with the marketplace more or less authentically, discerning distinguishing existential needs from merely created or artificial wants. Nevertheless, while the authenticity ideal aims to uphold our free agency, it runs the risk of being a mirage or chimera that we never fully realize. Even the more mundane versions suggested (meaningful work and life-giving relationships) are beyond the reach for many. Most of us find ourselves immersed in circumstances with family, friends, and work that do not reflect our authentic (or wholly autonomous) choices. We are often not able to disengage from such socially shaped commitments to pursue personal authenticity, nor do we often want to. This brings us to an apparent dead end: Authenticity is the cure for existential boredom, and it is beyond reach for most of us. Svendsen describes our predicament accordingly:

> So we would appear to be in an impossible situation, where we neither can seek the meaning we need within ourselves nor in anything outside ourselves—in fashion, for example. Without such a meaning, we search for every conceivable kind of meaning-substitute outside ourselves, but we are well aware that they never last. To get rid of this lack of duration we are always on the lookout for something new, so as to keep things going as long as possible. (2008, p. 79)

Existential boredom, Svendsen contends, simply "has to be accepted as an unavoidable fact, as life's own gravity" (p. 154). While sympathetic with Heidegger's analysis, Svendsen also is doubtful that authenticity can serve as an ersatz metaphysical placeholder in the place of traditional meaning structures that have lost appeal for many. Authenticity or personal meaning, Svendsen contends, "turns out to be unrealizable. We can quite well wait a life-time for this meaning, but it never comes" (p. 154). All we can hope for, Svendsen contends, are small moments of meaning, punctuated by a lot of situational and existential boredom. Yes, we can try to escape this conundrum via bold maneuvers (e.g., sky-diving, drugs) but such attempts, which are often reckless or require new extremes to be effective, prove to be temporary, leaving us more bereft after each attempt.

Svendsen's conclusion is compelling, offering what appears to be a realistic, albeit stark, assessment. To the child or young adult who complains about existential boredom, Svendsen's reply essentially amounts to the familiar parental retort, "That's life, get used to it." There is no grand solution, Svendsen contends, "for the problem of boredom has none" (2008, p. 154). This is essentially where the French existentialist philosopher Albert Camus (1913–1960) lands in the "The Myth of Sisyphus." Life is absurd and often boring, and we should, like Sisyphus, simply persist with it, letting go of attempts to find meaning or greater significance. Sisyphus' plight sounds abysmal (endlessly pushing a rock up a hill over and over again, only to watch it perpetually tumble to the bottom), and yet this tedium, Camus notes, is true of so much modern work, which is no less absurd. Camus, though, imagines Sisyphus heroically accepting and thereby owning his fate. Sisyphus sees with utter clarity the absurdity of existence, and its futile tedium, and yet he embraces it all the same. He does not expect or look for ultimate meaning.

To Kierkegaard's protest that if this is all there is – a "bottomless void" of dreary repetition – then "what would life be but despair?" Camus calmly responds, yes life is despair, "seeking what is true is not seeking what is desirable (1979, p. 43)." We may recoil from despair, desiring ultimate meaning, but for the French existentialist, there none is to be found. Sisyphus is heroic because he accepts this fate. The alternative, Camus contends, requires an irrational leap to imbue the ordinary with transcendental significance. Doing so is, Camus avers, to live like a donkey, which feeds "on the roses of illusion" (p. 43). "The struggle itself toward the heights," Camus declares, "is enough to fill a man's heart" (p. 49). "One must," Camus concludes, "imagine Sisyphus happy" (p. 111).

For such thinkers, we need to let go of attempts to decipher or extract transcendental meaning or significance from the phenomenon of existential boredom. There is, as Svendsen suggests, not much more to see here. In fact, attempts to fathom the ultimate meaning or significance of existential boredom give it undue power. We are unreasonably demanding, Svendsen contends, "capital letters where we are obliged to make do with small ones" (2008, p. 154). Even though there is "no Meaning given," there are little meanings (p. 154). There is also genuine boredom, and like Sisyphus, we should triumphantly embrace this fate. The claim is that we need to let go of our desire for Meaning writ large, and settle for small, ephemeral moments of meaning.

Camus begins his provocative essay on Sisyphus by claiming that there "is but one truly serious philosophical problem, and that is suicide. Judging whether life is or is not worth living amounts to answering the fundamental question of philosophy" (1979, p. 11). What begins as an intriguing inquiry into the meaning of life, and a summons for philosophy to take seriously this quest for meaning and purpose, ends with an "enlightened" resignation and acceptance that there is no significant meaning or purpose to life, apart from our own willful acceptance of or rejection of it. We are, like the protagonist of *Groundhog Day*, mired within an endless and seemingly pointless repetition.[9] At best, all we can hope for is to perform tasks or endure situations that are more, rather than less stimulating. Instead of grinding work and crass pleasures, life might consist of a comfortable desk job and refined pleasures.

Camus' conclusion is problematic for two key reasons. First, it leads to a complacency vis-à-vis existential boredom. Like moods that come and go, all we can or should do when we face boredom is wait it out, resisting extreme or desperate attempts to remediate it. Second, and related to this first point, this conclusion eviscerates this phenomenon of moral significance. There is not much more at stake or to be gleaned from boredom. Regarding existential boredom, there is no riddle to be solved. It simply is! If this is the case, then the two strategies noted in the introduction (avoidance and resignation) are simply the only options we have. Education that takes boredom seriously, then, involves largely discerning which strategy to employ, given the circumstances, and how

---

[9] This is the first, yet seemingly endless stage of the Phil Connor's (the protagonist of *Groundhog Day*), struggle with existential boredom. There is an illuminating pathway out of this dreary phase, which I explore in my Chapter 6.

we can steer clear of problematic boredom avoidance tendencies, especially addiction.

And yet, I think there is much more to glean from boredom. At a minimum, boredom indicates something is amiss, either with our environment or within ourselves. Contending with a boring situation, we often seek affirmation, checking in with others to see if they too find this activity, task, or job boring. Perhaps if they disagree with our assessment, we might begin to question our own judgment. For example, I find the game of chess to be boring, but I have friends who find it to be endlessly interesting. I can imagine if I were to talk with a friend about why they enjoy playing chess, they could begin to show me what there is to see. What appears to offer little engagement to my bored mind turns out to be far more complex, subtle, even dramatic. This is true of countless activities, situations, and persons. This example reveals that my bored mind is not simply a passive or objective condition I endure but the result of a willed volition – a willful inattention to certain possibilities at hand.

Like other mood states, boredom is shaped by our cognitive assessment (ways of thinking and seeing), which can often be abrupt, if not arrogant, in dismissing situations, activities, and other people as boring. More than a mood that happens to us, boredom is a state of mind that we assent to – a willful inattention to what is before us. In this simple example, the moral significance of boredom (as a willful lack of attention) comes into view. Psychologists continue to refine our conceptual and empirical understanding of this mood state, but an appreciation of the moral dimensions of this phenomenon has waned over time (Elpidorou, 2018).

Historically, boredom was understood as a moral emotion, especially its precursor acedia. Acedia is essentially the same condition moderns experience with boredom (with its characteristic restlessness and aimlessness), but it understands and interprets differently. Acedia translates as a lack (a-) of care (kedos). To suffer with acedia is to let oneself go – to become careless about one's interior life. Mercurial and under the radar, acedia was described as the "noon-day devil" because it strikes, unawares, in broad daylight. Given how seemingly innocuous it at first appears (as a mild listlessness with what we are doing), it is all too easy for it to take refuge in our mind and heart without even realizing it. What today we often simply regard as a passing malaise that we can abate with distraction, Evagrius viewed as a state of mind, a train of thought, that we should view with moral trepidation. Though far subtler than emotions like anger or fear, acedia was regarded as far more dangerous, because it is the breeding ground for a multitude of other sins, including greed, envy, and sloth. This account from Evagrius illustrates how this works:

> [Acedia] alone of all the thoughts is an entangled struggle of hate and desire. For the listless one hates whatever is in front of him and desires what is not. And the more desire drags the monk down, the more hate chases him out of his cell. He looks like an irrational beast, dragged by desire, and beat from behind by hate.... And further, [acedia] instils in him a dislike for the place and for his state of life itself, for manual labour, and also the idea that love has disappeared from among the brothers and there is no one to console him. And should there be someone during those days who has offended the monk, this too the demon uses to add further to his dislike (of the place). (Bunge, 2011, pp. 31 and 38)

This trajectory of thinking resonates with modern accounts of boredom, which so often lead to irritation, anger, and attempts to placate restless desires. Evagrius, however, does not end here. He urges the monks to keep up the struggle – to resist. If the monk is able to preserve, and fend off the multitude of urges that arise, the state of acedia eventually subsides and is followed by "a state of peace and ineffable joy." (p. 31).

This perspective of regarding boredom as a serious moral problem needs to be restored. Boredom is a mood state that involves interpretative judgments or ways of thinking and seeing. In order to assess it rightly, we need the right hermeneutic or interpretive key to make sense of it. This moral vision is needed now to both properly diagnose boredom and to provide a vision for how to best contend with it. To do this, I turn to Kierkegaard in Chapter 3.

3 DESPAIR
The Source of Boredom

The powerlessness to respond to the question, "What's the use?" or even the powerlessness to endure it, illustrates the supremely ruthless vanity of vanity, does it not? Nothing resists vanity since it can still skirt and annul all evidence, all certainty, all resistance. – Jean-Luc Marion (2006, p. 19).

Introduction

French philosopher Jean-Luc Marion changes the fundamental question in philosophy from Descartes', "How do I know I exist?" to "What's the use?" or "Why should I even care about existence?" This stultifying question points to the problem of existential boredom. Profound boredom calls into question the reason and motive for existing in the first place. It is a potential abyss that can swallow up all of life's purposes and initiatives. Marion's question resonates with Kierkegaard's claim that boredom "rests upon the nothing that interlaces existence" (1987, p. 291). This sounds like where Camus lands, noting the existential void that surrounds us, while encouraging us to make peace with it as best we can. This, however, is not where Kierkegaard concludes, but where he begins. Yet, it is not Kierkegaard who makes this observation about boredom but his pseudonym, A, the author of Part I of *Either/Or* (Poet A henceforth) (1843/1987). Kierkegaard is occasionally cited in boredom research, with the references usually drawn from Poet A, who offers witty reflections on the nature of boredom, lamenting his own struggle with boredom, yet considering himself to be especially profound given that he perceives the boredom that "interlaces" existence and knows how best to overcome it.[1]

Kierkegaard, however, did not intend for Poet A to be regarded as a trustworthy source, either for diagnosing or contending with boredom. Rather with Poet A Kierkegaard aimed to fashion a pseudonym that would attract readers to be more introspective about the nature of their own bored state. Poet A's reflections about boredom powerfully resonate with conventional intuitions. Yet rather than being captivated by Poet A's musings, Kierkegaard hoped his reader would recognize in A's state of being a wretched condition that should repulse them. Kierkegaard hoped his readers would be edified by it, rather than voyeuristic about Poet A's suffering. Kierkegaard hopes Poet A's misery will prompt serious existential reflection and ultimately a rejection of the strategies and maneuvers Poet A holds up as the optimal solution for contending with boredom.

Seeing through the vanity of A's solution, and desiring something better, Kierkegaard aimed to entice readers to read further, encountering his later pseudonyms, Johannes Climacus, Johannes de Silentio, and Anti-Climacus, the pseudonym of *Sickness unto Death* (1849/1983). Where pseudonym Poet A is portrayed as a brilliant, but immature protagonist, Anti-Climacus (AC henceforth) is depicted as a wise and experienced elder. Although amusing and interesting, Poet A is confused about the nature of his condition. He misdiagnoses the deeper causes of boredom and is thereby misguided about how best to contend with it. What Poet A holds up as the best alternative for contending with boredom, AC exposes as fraught with despair.

Boredom, which to Poet A first appears to be a mood state wrought by dull circumstances, AC reveals to be conditioned by an underlying despair that afflicts the human condition – a despair that we often unwittingly nurture and hold on to. AC's framework reveals the dynamics of boredom and how we remain mired within it; and it illuminates a constructive response to boredom. AC draws from ancient sources for understanding this mood state. While

---

[1] See, for example, Danckert and Eastwood (2020) and Svendsen (2008).

Kierkegaard talks about the term boredom in the modern sense that we are familiar with, he connects this mood state to deeper currents within the Christian tradition, especially to the vice of acedia. Though boredom is a modern construct, Kierkegaard discerns the timeless phenomenon it aims to capture and the stirrings of despair that are within it.

In this chapter, I begin by considering Poet A – a compelling representative of how we usually understand and respond to this mood state. A's account reveals three key facets of boredom: the incessant striving of our voracious ego, the onset of existential fatigue, and our ever-resilient attempts to fend off boredom, seeking both to maximize freedom and maintain control. I then turn to AC's analysis. Rather than understanding boredom as a neutral mood state that comes and goes, AC diagnoses it as laced with forms of despair that easily overtakes us. When we maneuver to escape this kind of boredom, we only become further mired in it. AC's framework illuminates and brings conceptual depth and insight to the two dominant boredom responses I noted in the introduction, avoidance and resignation.

The Subject of Boredom

The beginning of Kierkegaard's official and public authorship begins with a person who is in the throes of existential boredom. This is why Kierkegaard is particularly valuable for this study. Though Poet A's plight is, in many ways, representative of the universal human struggle with boredom, he is not an average person. Instead, he is gifted with poetic skill and a penchant for intensive reflection. Poet A is an eloquent and witty interpreter of his experience. For Kierkegaard, boredom is an enduring and fundamental human problem. More than simply a mood state, boredom avoidance is a default setting. It constitutes a way of living, or what Kierkegaard describes as the aesthetic sphere. In continually making adjustments to steer clear of this painful mood, we are beholden to it, even as we are often unaware of this dynamic.

Poet A's musings can be divided roughly into two parts: diagnostic and constructive. The first section consists of assorted reflections as he ponders his drab state of mind. In the second section, Poet A provides strategies for combating boredom. Apparently, up to this point in his life, A has been a "successful" aesthete, adept at procuring and enjoying assorted pleasures. This strategy, though, has begun to run its course. The amusements and diversions that were once satisfying are no longer. His "eyes," he says, are "surfeited and bored with everything" and yet he still hungers (1987, p. 20). Caught in the snares of this state, he does not "feel like doing anything ... walking, riding, even lying down," for then he would have to "get up again" (1987, p. 20). He says that if he "were offered all the glories of the world or all the torments of the world, one would move me no more than the other; I would not turn over to the other side either to attain or to avoid" (p. 37). To Poet A everything feels redundant, if not pointless. His soul, he reports, "is so heavy that no thought can carry it any longer, no wing beat can lift it up into the ether any more" (p. 29). He goes on, further noting that his "soul is dull and slack; in vain do I jab the spur of desire into its side; it is exhausted, it can no longer raise itself up in its royal jump. I have lost all my illusions" (p. 41). While a committed aesthete, or pleasure-maximizer, Poet A has reached a dead-end. To be clear, this is not clinical depression. He is capable of going through the motions and keeping up a front while this bored state roils within. Moreover, he is hopeful he will find the right mix of strategies to keep boredom at bay.

Poet A embodies the logical endpoint of boredom avoidance via pleasure. Most of us, he notes, are happily oblivious – moving from one pleasure to next, avoiding the severe redundancy fatigue that Poet A is experiencing. However, once we, like A, become conscious of this cycle, unsettling questions are sure to follow: "What is the point of all this?" "Is life really just insufferably boring?" What is striking in Poet A's account, and other accounts of existential boredom, is the metaphysical speculation that it prompts. Poet A does not simply render judgment about his own condition but also about the nature and meaning of the universe itself. While modern psychological accounts of boredom aim to steer clear of metaphysical speculation, the subject, or boredom sufferer, often cannot resist being drawn into a metaphysical quagmire. Worse still, this bleak vision can feel as if it is a true revelation of the world as it simply is: cold and indifferent. Poet A's grim metaphysical assessment echoes Schopenhauer's claim that boredom is "proof that existence has no real value in itself; for what is boredom but the feeling of the emptiness of life?" (1851/2008, p. 15).

Poet A is situationally and existentially bored through and through. He is also acutely aware of his situation – he sees with eyes wide open the abyss that awaits beneath the noise and distraction. Poet A is too self-conscious, too self-reflective, to ignore or shut out this underlying pain. The strategies that work for most people – keeping busy with a steady stream of gossip, hobbies, news, tawdry pleasures, and so on – do not work for him. In many respects, Poet A sounds a lot like Qoheleth in Ecclesiastes, raving about the vanity and pointlessness of everything under the sun. Yet while Qoheleth is somehow able to affirm the meaningfulness of the universe, A cannot. He can only see himself and everything as submerged in a sea of nothingness.

While Poet A understands how boredom avoidance permeates all of our activities, he believes that there is nothing more to life than this. We are condemned to this fate, whether we are conscious of it or not. We are Sisyphus, stuck in an endless loop. Yet, Poet A does not accept Sisyphus' peaceful, though bleak, resignation. Even though he is caught within the confines of this repetitive grind, A is hopeful there are better and worse ways to contend with and stave off boredom. There are tactics and strategies, he recommends, to make even the dreariest situations interesting. Yes, boredom avoidance is all there is, but A promises to reveal superior boredom avoidance strategies that keep the abyss at bay. Seeking too quickly to escape boredom, he notes, will only deepen its hold on us.

Counterintuitively, Poet A advises taking up what he describes as the "rotation of crops" (p. 291). This idea is often misunderstood as changing the soil, which is interpreted to mean that the solution to boredom is continually changing our situation (via travel, new jobs, new friends, and so on). We hope to overcome boredom through extending our range of options, but this approach, Poet A notes, offers what he describes as a "spurious infinity" (p. 292). When confronted with situational boredom (usually characterized by an unstimulating and restrictive environment), we instinctively long for escape, to watch the clock, or to sulk in the moment, with increasing agitation.

What we need instead is to limit our options. This, Poet A explains, is what "true rotation of crops" consists of (p. 291). It does not involve changing the soil but changing the "method of cultivation and the kinds of crops" (p. 292). This process is intensive, rather than extensive; it is informed by what Poet A describes as the sole saving principle, "the principle of limitation" (p. 292). "The more a person limits himself," A notes, "the more resourceful he becomes" (p. 292). Facing boredom, we often seek to maximize rather than minimize limitations. Yet, the move to maximize options only deepens our bored state and our frustration. Limitation, A advises, is precisely what we need so as to prod our imagination to see possibilities for engagement that previously appeared fallow.

To illustrate how this principle works, Poet A invites us to recollect our school days, "when there was no esthetic consideration in the choosing of our teachers, and therefore they were often very boring—how resourceful we were then! What fun we had catching a fly, keeping it prisoner under a nutshell, and watching it run around with it!" (p. 292). The more a person limits herself, A notes, the more resourceful she becomes: "to [her] a spider can be a source of great amusement" (p. 292). This form of relief is "not through extensity but through intensity" (p. 292). The key to enacting this principle is exorcising hope – hope that the boring circumstance will end soon. Facing boredom, we instinctively check the time and count the minutes until the situation ends. This is a form of hoping and not until such hope has been dashed, A instructs, can "one begin to live artistically; as long as a person hopes, he cannot limit himself" (p. 292). "Hope exposes the hopeful to the possibility of frustration" (Mackey, 1971, p. 10). The way to relinquish hope, A counsels, is to marvel at nothing, that is to say, no part of life "ought to have so much meaning for a person that he cannot forget it any moment he wants to; on the other hand, every single part of life ought to have so much meaning for a person that he can remember it at any moment" (p. 293). The natural hierarchy of experiences that cause wonder is displaced by a leveling trivialization of everything.

Once we thus limit ourselves, the imagination is thereby primed to see possibilities for amusement that were hitherto unrecognized. Poet A shares the story of being held captive to someone droning on endlessly:

> On the verge of despair, I suddenly discovered that the man perspired exceptionally much when he spoke. This perspiration now absorbed my attention. I watched how the

> pearls of perspiration collected on his forehead, then united
> in a rivulet, slid down his nose, and ended in a quivering
> globule that remained suspended at the end of his nose.
> From that moment on, everything was changed; I could
> even have the delight of encouraging him to commence his
> philosophical instruction just in order to watch the perspi-
> ration on his brow and on his nose. (p. 299)

This occasion is utterly arbitrary, and this arbitrariness, notes A,
is "the whole secret" that enables one to enjoy "something totally
accidental" (p. 299). This move is all too familiar in the internet
age, where odd, seemingly nonsensical memes catch and spread like
wildfire, amassing millions of views within a few days.

While the limiting principle applies to situations in
which we are stuck, Poet A recommends avoiding stagnant situations and arrangements that limit options as much as possible.
Never, A says, "become involved in *marriage*. If an individual
is to marry, he has lost his freedom and cannot order his riding
boots when he wishes, cannot knock about according to whim"
(pp. 296–297). "Moreover, through marriage one falls into a very
deadly continuity with custom, and custom is like the wind and
weather, something completely indeterminable" (p. 297). The
limiting principle, it turns out, is only for desperate situations – a
stop-gap measure for those inevitably dull situations in which we
find ourselves. Otherwise, A recommends living without limits as
much as possible. Toward this end, Poet A advises against taking
an official post of any kind. "If one does that, one becomes just
a plain John Anyman, a tiny little cog in the machine of the body
politic" (p. 298).

This capacity for existential whimsy is what A cherishes
most, hence he stays clear of official posts that might involve real
responsibility. Instead, he attaches "great importance to all the
pursuits that are compatible with aimlessness" (p. 298). In particular, he notes that teasing "is an excellent means of exploration"
(p. 299). Though A cannot control circumstances or moods, "he
can determine the meaning these circumstances will have for him
by the practice of systematic arbitrariness" and thus, in this way,
maintain control (Mackey, 1971, p. 10). A also carefully steers
clear of moral attachments, which risk drawing him into tedious

obligations. He shows this strategy at work when encountering a homeless person:

> What a strange, sad mood came over me on seeing a poor wretch shuffling through the streets in a somewhat worn pale green coat flecked with yellow. I felt sorry for him, but nevertheless what affected me most was that the color of this coat so vividly reminded me of my childhood's first production in the noble art of painting. Is it not sad that these color combinations, which I still think of with so much joy, are nowhere to be found in life; the whole world finds them crude, garish, suitable only for Nürnberg prints. (Kierkegaard, 1987, p. 23)

A's thoughts, initially moved by the tragic condition of this individual, quickly skip to a trivial association, avoiding clear of the ethical challenge this person's plight might pose.

This simple example contains a devastating social commentary. Boredom avoidance often eclipses ethical possibilities. We are often more inclined to avoid the pain of boredom than alleviate the pain of others. Considering the prospect of having to go to church, Poet A also finds clever ways to keep himself entertained and avoid any ethical injunctions. Instead of listening to the pastor's sermon, he directs his attention to aesthetic considerations (e.g., the pastor's manner of speaking or dress). What might be yet another occasion of ethical edification Poet A skips over, ever steering his attention from the ethical to the trivial. He has honed the art of "seizing the occasion—any occasion—and turning it to capricious ends," thus making and unmaking "the situation as it pleases him" (Mackey, 1971, p. 11). Poet A can discover in the most mundane and barren circumstances fuel for his amusement.

A's reflections reveal three key facets at work in the bored mind. The first is that the struggle with boredom is fundamentally a struggle to appease a voracious ego that craves both *constant stimulation and control* over its circumstances. The second facet is the existential fatigue that awaits as escapist amusements lose their charm. This can occasion an existential crisis, as is the case for Poet A. What Poet A previously found engaging and stimulating, he now finds to be bankrupt and dull. This is coupled with a metaphysical gloom. The third facet is the resilience of the ego. Assuming that we are not afflicted with pathological depression, the rotation of crops method is essentially a doubling down on escapism, finding new, innovative ways to escape the moment. Kierkegaard would immediately recognize the fragmented, episodic, and endless amusement afforded by contemporary social media as the aesthetic modality writ large. We are continually poised for the next arbitrary source of amusement and distraction.

Poet A cannot see or imagine an alternative way of being, apart from boredom avoidance. The idea of being a dull ordinary person repulses him. Poet A is also not animated by the ideal of authenticity – a commitment to being true to himself. Rather than striving to be a self, the aesthetic modality is characterized by escaping from the self. Becoming a self requires enacting a possibility and committing to it. Every choice is a renunciation of every other choice. Instead, Poet A strives to hold onto possibility, thus treading in place. More than a longing for wealth or power, Poet A wishes "for the passion of possibility, for the eternally young, eternally ardent, that sees possibility everywhere. Pleasure disappoints; possibility does not. And what wine is so sparkling, so fragrant, so intoxicating!" (p. 41). I now turn to Kierkegaard's *Sickness unto Death* for deeper insight into A's condition.

Sickness unto Death: Diagnosing Despair

It is this avoidance of becoming a self that the author of the *Sickness* diagnoses as the fundamental root of Poet A's struggle, which is the underlying problem with boredom avoidance. More than boredom, A suffers with despair, which he feels acutely but is unable to name or understand. Despair, AC contends, is universal. "There is not one single living human being," AC observes,

> who does not despair a little, who does not secretly harbor an unrest, an inner strife, a disharmony, an anxiety about an unknown something or a something he does not even dare to try to know, an anxiety about some possibility in existence or an anxiety about himself. (1983, p. 22)

It is this underlying despair that makes boredom particularly noxious. Alone with our thoughts, we might catch a glimpse of this. T. S. Eliot captures this dynamic in *The Four Quartets*. Describing a moment on a delayed train with strangers, he notes how the conversation rose and then fell "into silence" (1971, p. 28). He then observed how behind every face, one could see "the mental emptiness deepen / Leaving only the growing terror of nothing to think about" (p. 28). This terror is pure boredom, not just situational boredom (which will pass once the train arrives) but also the more troubling phenomenon of existential boredom – the realization that life ultimately is meaningless. AC contends that boredom, which often appears to be an external problem, is primarily an internal problem. The bored self is a disordered, despairing self. To understand this, AC's incisive yet disorienting definition of a human being merits quoting in full:

> A human being is spirit. But what is spirit? Spirit is the self. But what is the self? The self is a relation that relates itself to itself or is the relation's relating itself to itself in the relation; the self is not the relation but is the relation's relating itself to itself. A human being is a synthesis of the infinite and the finite, of the temporal and the eternal, of freedom and necessity, in short a synthesis. (p. 13)

Consistent with traditional anthropological conceptions, AC sees a human being as composed of two parts: a body and a soul. Yet, AC's use of the category of spirit, in contrast to soul, underscores a dynamic understanding of the human person. With the language of "spirit" and "relation's relating," AC emphasizes the self as a constant work in progress.[2] There is no standing self; there is no true or deeper self, but rather a continual becoming (or unbecoming) insofar as the self relates "itself to itself."

The proper self-synthesis consists of balancing the two major parts of the self, the infinite and the finite. By infinite or possibility, AC is referring to the ability to imagine possibilities for self-becoming. This capacity is a lens that needs to be used with caution. Infinitude or possibility, while it is a lens that enables the self to imagine becoming a better self, is untruthful in that the self one sees is not one's actual

---

[2] Walter Davis, though in a different context, captures this insight: "No depth exists in the subject until it is created. No a priori identity awaits us.... Inwardness is a process of becoming, a work, the labour of the negative. The self is not a substance one unearths by peeling away layers until one gets to the core, but an integrity one struggles to bring into existence" (1989, p. 105).

self. In actuality, possibility is a nothing. By finite, Kierkegaard is referring to the physical limitations that come with being an embodied self – the brute facts or necessities of our material existence. Finitude, properly used, consists of recognizing what is truly possible for the self. It is an awareness of where one is, where one is starting from, where actuality and therefore existence can begin. Kierkegaard does not view the mind–soul part as the essential self, nor does he view the combination of the two parts (body–soul) to be the true self. Rather, the self is that which bridges the two parts; it is the "reflexive structure that transcends the first-order" body–soul relation (Davenport, 2012). Becoming an actual self involves properly harmonizing the two poles within the self. This is a never-ending task. To the extent that we veer toward finitude, on the one hand, or infinitude, on the other, the self suffers despair. Recall that Poet A praises possibility, but this is not possibility infused with hope, and measured by necessity. Rather, it is possibility used "as a diverting stimulant" seeking to be "diverted by the inconstant, futile, weird phantasmal flashes of possibility" (Kierkegaard et al., 1995, p. 254).

This overview perhaps sounds abstract, but it provides, as I intend to show, a powerful framework for illuminating the deeper struggle latent within our fight with boredom. The experience of existential boredom reveals despair, and boredom avoidance or resignation deepens despair. A simple way to understand this dialectic is to see infinitude or possibility as our capacity to imagine a better version of ourselves. Consider an alcoholic imagining a state of sobriety. The sober self is a potential self, but not an actual self. How important, though, is this capacity to imagine an alternative way of being? Yet, this possibility needs to be qualified and situated within the necessities of life – the daily routine, acquaintances, friends, and activities – that comprise this person's field of action. Only then might it lead to actuality. Imagination, though, is required for taking the first step. Without infinitude or possibility, all we have is finitude or restricting necessities, which appear unchangeable.[3]

---

[3] Mary Midgley, commenting on Iris Murdoch's (2014) view of the imagination, resonates with this understanding: "The imagination (that is) can itself be used to pierce and unweave the veil with which it has helped to blind us. It is not just a deluding factor or a luxury item to amuse humanists. It is itself a vital organ, a workshop where we forge our view of the world and thereby our actions" (p. xvi).

We often fail to strike the right balance, veering toward necessity, on the one hand, or possibility, on the other. We may also be unaware of this task of becoming altogether. In *Either/Or*, Kierkegaard shares the example of Don Juan who is so submerged within sensate categories (moving from one pleasure to the next) that he is completely oblivious to the task of becoming a self. Again, to use the metaphor of addiction, Don Juan is akin to an addict on the lookout for his next hit. Talk of self-becoming or self-overcoming does not make sense. Don Juan, in Kierkegaard's technical sense, is not a self but an animal seeking pleasure maximization.

To the degree that we avoid or fail to properly synthesize the parts of the self, we suffer despair – either the despair of infinitude (in which we become lost within a sea of unrealizable possibilities) or the despair of finitude (in which we cannot see anything beyond our cramped necessities). Whether we are conscious or unconscious of this failed synthesis of the self, we are in despair. Striking a balance between both is a delicate process. While habituation (or repetitive actions that strike the right balance) can become an ally, it can also become an obstacle, suggesting a false sense of stability or an illusion of a permanent self. This fragile dialectic reveals how vigilant we have to be, given the temptation or tendency to veer toward possibility or necessity. Although this discussion provides an initial account of what despair is, it remains still quite schematic. What does it really mean to fall out of step in the task of self-synthesis? What does it feel like to descend into despair? In what follows, I examine further the two major forms of despair that AC believes afflict the self, providing examples along the way.

Despair of Possibility

The formula for all despair is "to will to be rid of oneself" (Kierkegaard, 1983, p. 20). Despair is fundamentally an avoidance of the self that leads to a diminished self and a lack of self-agency. Despair, notes AC, is often misconstrued as despair over something, but ultimately despair is over the self. For instance, in wanting to be like someone else, one may despair over not being more like that person, but really this despair is despairing over the self one is and being stuck with that self. In short, despair wants to be rid of the self one is or affirm a self one is not.

To suffer the despair of infinitude (or possibility) is to be caught up in the fantastic mediated by the imagination. The person who despairs of possibility is prone to fantasizing about actions or vicariously living through the actions of others. To be clear, as noted, the capacity to imagine alternative existential possibilities is an essential and vital part of becoming a self. It enables an ability to reflect and, as noted, and imagine the possibility of becoming a better self. Yet often rather than imagine viable possibilities for ourselves, we are drawn to voyeuristically track the possibilities that confront other selves. Consider the familiar phenomena of gawking at a car accident, or tracking the latest gossip. We are prone to entertain fanciful possibilities that do not pertain to the self's edification or becoming. This form of despair, while stimulating, is ultimately a form of self-stagnation. Kierkegaard would not be surprised by the conspiracy theories that abound, as such theories divert attention away from difficult task of forging our own self, drawing us into the machinations of other imagined selves. What such theories provide is a cozy place to dwell in fantastical possibilities. In part, the inability to counter such fantasies with factual proof is due to the fact that it is a comfortable form of despair. Again, self-becoming is a constant task. Living vicariously or taking in conspiracy theories we evade this task.

The despair of infinitude, as it progresses, continues to lead a person away from themselves. In which case we imagine ourselves being a certain way or being a certain kind of person (e.g., generous), yet this ideal is utterly fantastical and removed from our actual mode of being. Dostoevsky's elder Zossima in *The Brothers Karamazov* offers a poignant account of the despair of possibility. He recounts a story about a doctor who embodies this version of despair. Confiding in the elder, the doctor shares:

> the more I love humankind in general, the less I love people in particular, that is, individually, as separated persons. In my dreams.... I often went so far as to think passionately of serving humankind, and, it may be, would really have

gone to the cross for people if it were somehow suddenly necessary, and yet I am incapable of living in the same room with anyone even for two days. (1992, pp. 57–58)

When unchecked, the despair of possibility revels in possibilities, but possibilities take time to be actualized. This time is not taken, and before actualizing a possibility, new possibilities emerge, and the "time that should be used for actuality grows shorter and shorter; everything becomes more and more momentary" (Kierkegaard, 1983, p. 36). Becoming a self requires concrete actualization. The despair of possibility avoids actual existence, escaping into flights of fancy, all the while delaying action.

Augustine's famous plea captures this dynamic. Mired in degradation he prays to God, "Give me chastity and continence," with his despairing self then interceding to say, "only not yet" (p. 198). While Augustine can imagine a better self, he stalls at the prospect of living into it. In Augustine's case (at this point in his journey), possibility outruns necessity. The "self becomes an abstract possibility; it flounders in possibility but neither moves from the place where it is nor arrives anywhere, for necessity is literally that place; to become oneself is literally a movement in that place" (Kierkegaard, 1983, p. 36). Augustine continues to imagine a better self, but his impotence (inability and unwillingness to merge a different possibility with his concrete necessities) leads to getting lost in countless possibilities, failing to take the time to actualize any one of them. The self enamored of countless possibilities lacks actuality. "What is missing," notes AC, "is not a lack of energy but the power to obey, to submit to the necessity of one's life, to what may be called one's limitations" (p. 36). Pascal offers a clear explanation of this kind of despair: "We do not content ourselves with the life we have in ourselves and in our own being; we desire to live an imaginary life in the mind of others, and for this purpose we endeavour to shine. We labour unceasingly to adorn and preserve this imaginary existence, and neglect the real" (2018, p. 31).

To better understand the despair of possibility, it is helpful to see what overcoming it looks like. A recent obituary about the pianist Leon Fleischer captures this movement. Fleischer was a piano prodigy, debuting at Carnegie Hall at the age of 16. Yet at the age of 36, he suffered a mysterious neurological affliction that essentially crippled his right hand and nearly ended his career. None of the treatments he received helped, and Fleischer fell into a 2-year period of despair, to the point of considering suicide. But then, an epiphany: as Fleischer put it, "I suddenly came to the realization that my connection with music was greater than just as a two-handed piano player." Fleischer essentially re-invented himself, becoming a teacher, a conductor, and a performer of the left-handed repertoire for piano. (Pies, 2020)

As Thomas Moore put it, "it was the expansion of his musical vision that saved him" (Pies, 2020). In Kierkegaardian terms, Fleischer was able to strike a balance between necessity (recognizing limitations without being wholly determined by them) and possibility for self-becoming.

Despair of Necessity

The despair of necessity (or finitude) is, simply put, to lack infinitude or possibility. This involves a narrow reductionism, a complete acceptance of a worldly mentality. Consumed by everyday matters, AC says that such a "person forgets himself, forgets his name divinely understood, does not dare to believe in himself, finds it too hazardous to be himself and far easier and safer to be like others, to become a copy, a number, a mass man" (Kierkegaard, 1983, p. 33). Such a person, by losing herself in this way, may be very successful in the world, always playing it safe, counting on probabilities. Yet, she never ventures in the highest sense. She mortgages herself to the world. William Deresiewicz describes a version of this kind of despair permeating Ivy League schools: "The system manufactures students who are smart and talented and driven, yes, but also anxious, timid, and lost, with little intellectual curiosity and a stunted sense of purpose: trapped in a bubble of privilege, heading meekly in the same direction, great at what they're doing but with no idea why they're doing it" (2014, p. 2). The anxieties of maintaining worldly security totally consume the heart. Kierkegaard's account, via AC, clearly foreshadows Heidegger's vision of the inauthentic self, subsumed within the crowd.

At its extreme to despair of necessity is to slide into a complacent fatalism. A prevailing example of this outlook is what Kierkegaard describes as the philistine-bourgeois mentality. "Bereft of imagination, as the philistine-bourgeois always is, whether ale-house keeper or prime minister, he lives within a certain trivial compendium of experience as to how things go, what is possible, what usually happens" (Kierkegaard, 1983, p. 41). Weighed down by necessity, we submit ourselves to the "parrot-wisdom of routine experience," as AC puts it (Kierkegaard, 1983, p. 40). A clear example of this, G. K. Chesterton notes, is when an older business person "rebukes the idealism" of an office intern saying something to the effect like so: "Ah, yes, when one is young, one has these ideals in the abstract and these castles in the air; but in middle age they all break up like clouds, and one comes down to a belief in practical politics, to using the machinery one has and getting on with the world as it is" (1908, p. 25).

The despair of necessity is often characterized by restraint, holding back, playing it safe. A person, AC notes, "regrets ten times for having spoken to once for having kept silent" (1983, p. 33). In maintaining such silence and playing it safe, we fail to venture out, to test out possibilities. By "maintaining silence, a person is thrown wholly upon himself; here actuality does not come to his aid" (p. 34). "If I have ventured wrongly," AC notes, "well, then life helps me by punishing me. But if I have not ventured at all, who helps me then?" (p. 34). Thus, this despair of necessity flies under the radar unseen, residing within the heart of the single individual hiding in the crowd.

Without possibility and infinity, we lack worthy ideals to aspire to and actualize – finitude and necessity become flat and narrow. Simone Weil (1909–1943) recounts what the despair of necessity looks like first hand. As a young and idealistic Marxist, Weil quit her teaching job to work on an assembly line at the *Renault* car factory for a year. Her aim was to comprehend firsthand the necessities faced by blue collar workers. In her journals, she describes the physical exhaustion and social alienation she experienced, noting the limited time allotted to meaningfully interact with her coworkers. As she persisted, she increasingly found herself incapable of explaining and critically understanding her situation. More than this, Weil notes the intellectual deprivation brought on by the monotonous yet stressful tasks that consumed her attention. Considering her coworkers, she notes that when they

> complain, they almost always complain in superficial terms, without voicing the nature of the true discontent.... Workingmen themselves do not find it easy to write, speak, or even reflect on such a subject, for the first effect of suffering is the attempt of thought to escape. It refuses to confront the adversity that wounds it. Thus, when workingman [sic] speak of their lot, they repeat more often than not the catchwords coined by people who are not workingmen. (Weil and Panichas, 1977, p. 64)

Not only did Weil observe this plight in her peers, but she also found herself struggling with this same phenomenon. This inability to name one's own experience (except with cliches that are handed down), coupled with resignation, is the crux of the despair of necessity. Such tedium, which is at first infuriating in its monotony, "eventually passes into a necessity that is accepted with indifference, until even the sense of dissatisfaction with the pure functionalism of the task is lost" (Treanor, 2021).

Elsewhere, Weil recounts another striking example of the despair of necessity. Her older brother André Weil, was a math prodigy and later became an influential mathematician. Though intellectually gifted herself, Weil found it difficult to live under her brother's shadow. She shares the following story:

> At fourteen I fell into one of those fits of bottomless despair that come with adolescence, and I seriously thought of dying because of the mediocrity of my natural faculties. The exceptional gifts of my brother, who had a childhood and youth comparable to those of Pascal, brought my own inferiority home to me. I did not mind having no visible successes, but what did grieve me was the idea of being excluded from that transcendent kingdom to which only the truly great have access and wherein truth abides. I preferred to die rather than live without that truth. (1951, p. 6)

Weil sees a brilliant possibility for someone else that it is not available to her. Her limitations (in particular, a mind less capable than her brother's for mathematical prowess) is cause for her despair.

Again, the formula for despair is self-loathing, and we see this acutely in Weil's case. In this particular case, she is contending with the despair of necessity. Despondent about her lack of gifts compared to her brother, she is unable to recognize the gifts she does have, thus eclipsing viable possibilities.

Weil's state of despair persists, yet after months of "inward darkness" she suddenly arrives

> at the everlasting conviction that any human being, even though practically devoid of natural faculties, can penetrate to the kingdom of truth reserved for genius, if only he longs for truth and perpetually concentrates all his attention upon its attainment. He thus becomes a genius too, even though for lack of talent his genius cannot be visible from outside. (1951, p. 6)

Weil's transition (from despair to hope that becomes realized) is striking. In the middle of her despair – that is, on the precise point that was the cause of her existential turmoil – she comes to a central epiphany. Weil is able to find the resources to overcome her psychological limitations. She realizes that the "kingdom of truth" is a possibility for her and for everyone. This internal struggle AC recognizes as the "battle of faith, battling, madly, if you will, for possibility, because possibility is the only salvation" (Kierkegaard, 1983, p. 38). Weil's possibility, though, is grounded within her own particular necessities. It is not a fantastical pipe dream, but a recognition of the agency that is within her power – her ability to develop her own unique grasp of truth.

Conclusion

At this point, it is helpful to recount AC's diagnosis. First, AC takes it as axiomatic that despair is universal. The key distinction is not whether or not we are in despair, but the degree to which we are conscious of this fact or not. Despair is fundamentally a mis-relation within the self that takes two basic forms: the despair of possibility (which correlates to boredom avoidance) and the despair of necessity (which correlates to boredom resignation). Confronted with boredom we often veer toward possibilities, seeking to escape from the constraints and necessities of a particular situation. Or conversely, we resign ourselves to this situation as simply bereft of possibility thus relinquishing our agency. Striking the right synthesis of possibility and necessity is a never-ending task, which we often stumble at. Moreover, it is not an act we can accomplish and take pride in. With the self, AC reminds us, there is no standing still.

While despair is awful, it is evidence of our supreme stature vis-à-vis other animals. Because of our extraordinary capacity for possibility – this ability to imagine better ways of being – we are at risk of suffering despair. Squirrels do not despair, nor do they suffer with boredom. Boredom and despair, as possibilities for human beings, are also evidence of our great potential, of our particular excellence. While boredom is often painful, even, miserable, it alerts us to the self's need for movement – for a constant actualization.

What does the self without despair look like? This is the question that animates Chapter 4. What is an optimal synthesis of both necessity and possibility together? This is the framework for human flourishing that Kierkegaard holds up. Confronted with boredom, we face weary necessities, and we grope for new possibilities. Yet, in doing so, we often unwittingly exacerbate the despair we are seeking to alleviate. The move for possibility, though it risks being fanciful, is nevertheless infused with agency. This is especially true in the case of Poet A – he is not going to give up the struggle for new possibilities. Yet, what is lacking in A is an inability to surrender to the necessities before him and thereby to be open to them on their own terms. In pursuing genuine leisure, as I will argue, we are aiming to balance possibilities with necessities.

4 LEISURE
A Cure for Boredom

Introduction

Thus far, I have explored the distinction between situational and existential boredom. Existential boredom is a form of despair. While situational boredom usually has a clear and immediate source, the cause of existential boredom is more difficult to locate. Attention to existential boredom must turn inward – to the despairing self. While modern conditions, especially the breakdown of traditional sources of meaning, the increase of tedious work wrought by industrialization, and the incessant oversaturation by digital media have accelerated the rise of existential boredom, it is not wholly determined by them. We have, as Kierkegaard illuminates, more agency than we realize.

Nevertheless, our propensity for existential boredom is not simply a personal choice or a cultural predilection, but rather is a constitutive part of the human condition. The self, as Kierkegaard argues, is an unstable combination of possibility and necessity. As previously explained, despair and existential boredom can arise when we veer too much toward possibility or necessity, even as we are often unaware of this dynamic.

Here, true leisure is examined as a promising antidote to existential boredom, offering a middle way between what Kierkegaard defines as the despair of necessity and the despair of possibility. In contrast to amusement, genuine leisure does not come easily. Contrary to its popular usage as a synonym for rest and relaxation, leisure is far from a negative absence of effort. Rather, genuine leisure is an art that requires discipline, vigilance, and practice. As with other arts, amateurs or novices who are outsiders to the practice cannot appreciate or fully understand the goods it affords. It takes time, practice, and apprenticeship to become skilled enough at the art of leisure to experience the goods that are intrinsic to it.

First, let us examine the dynamics of contemporary so-called leisure, which is largely how we attempt to ameliorate boredom. To be sure, contemporary leisure is multifaceted, complex, and impossible to treat as monochromatic, yet there is an extensive leisure industry (entertainment like Disney and Netflix shows or cruises) that co-opts and gives shape and direction to how we envision what leisure is and what motivates it. For insight, I turn to David Foster Wallace's phenomenology of an iconic leisure event: the luxury cruise. Wallace's account illuminates the interior dynamics of contemporary leisure, examining what the self is undergoing in its pursuit of aesthetic diversions. Wallace reveals that what appears to offer self-renewal and self-actualization actually advances a form of blissful self-obliteration that enables the despair that Kierkegaard alerts us to.

I then turn to an alternative conception of leisure, which draws inspiration from classical sources. This tradition, which has evolved and developed in several cultural eras, traces a line from Aristotle to St. Benedict of Nursia to Thomas Aquinas up to more recent leisure visionaries, including Simone Weil and Josef Pieper. Rather than enhancing self-restoration, these writers contend, the vacancy and inaction of free time are prey to acedia – a spiritual and mental sloth. The classical leisure tradition takes direct aim at this tendency, cultivating practices of leisure which protect the self from falling into despair. The argument here is that contemporary leisure, as it is often understood and practiced, offers a temporary anesthetic that in the end intensifies existential boredom and despair. True leisure, by contrast, restores and renews the self, offering a powerful antidote to existential boredom and the despair that afflicts the self.[1, 2]

Wallace's Cruise: The Despair of Amusement

The turn to leisure perhaps sounds strange as a response to or cure for despair. To contemporary ears, leisure might sound too frivolous an answer to the self that has lost its way, suffering with

[1] Gary (2006)
[2] Gary (2017a)

malaise about meaning and purpose. Yet, this all hinges on how leisure is defined and practiced. Merriam-Webster defines leisure as the "freedom provided by the cessation of activities especially: time free from work or duties" (2021). Leisure, accordingly, is free time and space to do with what one pleases. The English word for leisure derives from the French *leisir*, which in turn is based on Latin *licere*, which means to "be allowed." Leisure's close cousin is the modern concept of a vacation, defined simply as "extended time for leisure." Deriving from the Latin *vacare*, vacation literally means to "be unoccupied" or "emptied out," as in vacuum. In short, modern leisure is defined and largely understood as what we choose to do after we have completed work and other obligations. Leisure is free time to relax and recover so we can then effectively resume work. While lacking substance itself, modern leisure's reference point is work. Aristotle's adage, "we work to be at leisure," has been reversed to, "we pursue leisure in order to work" (Pieper, 1998, p. 26).

How one chooses to spend their leisure time is prized as a matter of personal discretion. Nevertheless, while upholding the sanctity of autonomy, how we choose to spend our leisure time falls within a predictable range of activities. The leisure industry is a powerful economic engine that casts a compelling vision of what leisure is, what it promises to offer weary selves, and what kinds of activities constitute fruitful leisure.

The vacation cruise, in particular, stands out as an icon of modern leisure. It encompasses, all in one package, most of the trademark leisure activities that constitute what many contemporary people seek in modern leisure: voyeurism, partying, entertainment, sitting by the pool, eating out, playing games, and consuming alcohol – an endless bounty of options. And all of this is served up to cruise attendees by a fleet of workers, tirelessly attending to every passenger's whim. Wallace, in his essay "Shipping Out: On the (nearly lethal) comforts of a luxury cruise" offers an intensive reflection on the dynamics at play in this enterprise, exploring what happens to the self participating in this cruise leisure event spectacle. Toward this end, he went on a seven-day deluxe cruise with *Celebrity Cruises* (one of the premier cruise companies) to experience firsthand its many delights, all the while scrupulously observing himself and those around him.

More than simply a product or services, Wallace observed, Celebrity Cruises offering "something more like a feeling: a blend of relaxation and stimulation, stressless indulgence and frantic tourism, that special mix of servility and condescension that's marketed under configurations of the verb 'to pamper'" (Wallace, 1996, p. 34). Eavesdropping on fellow passengers in the waiting hangar, Wallace repeatedly heard passengers sharing their rationale for going on a cruise: relaxation. The self has to be "on" at work, to be responsive and professional. "I need time to relax" was the mantra Wallace heard repeatedly. This aligns with the modern view of leisure and vacation, as time to be unoccupied – nicely encapsulated by the "Do Not Disturb" sign on doors. The self wants to be left alone. This sounds ordinary enough, but it is significant. Anticipating leisure, the self anticipates and looks forward to a slackening of its intensity and agency. The self expects this, and to the extent that it is compromised, the self is disappointed.

To better understand the enticements of a cruise, Wallace begins with the advertising pitch itself – the cruise brochure. Wallace's analysis of this document merits quoting at length to illustrate how Celebrity seeks to enchant vacation-goers into its vision of splendid leisure:

> Just standing at the ship's rail looking out to sea has a profoundly soothing effect. As you drift along like a cloud on water, the weight of everyday life is magically lifted away, and you seem to be floating on a sea of smiles. Not just among your fellow guests but on the faces of the ship's staff as well. As a steward cheerfully delivers your drinks, you mention all of the smiles among the crew. He explains that every Celebrity [Cruise] staff member takes pleasure in making your cruise a completely carefree experience and treating you as an honored guest. Besides, he adds, there's no place else they'd rather be. Looking back out to sea, you couldn't agree more. (Wallace, 1996, p. 36)

The use of the second-person ("you drift"... "you mention"), Wallace notes, is peculiar yet intentional. It is "fantasy-enablement" with a disturbingly "authoritarian twist" (Wallace, 1996, p. 37). In spite of yourself, you will enjoy yourself! Celebrity Cruises will make sure, taking care of everything. Wallace elaborates:

[Celebrity Cruises] will micromanage every iota of every pleasure-option so that not even the dreadful corrosive action of your adult consciousness and agency and dread can fuck up your fun. Your troublesome capacities for choice, error, regret, dissatisfaction, and despair will be removed from the equation. You will be able–finally, for once to relax, the ads promise, because you will have no choice. Your pleasure will, for 7 nights and 6.5 days, be wisely and efficiently managed. Aboard the *Nadir*, as is ringingly foretold in the brochure, you will get to do "something you haven't done in a long, long time: Absolutely Nothing." (Wallace, 1996, p. 37)

The promise is not that "you can experience great pleasure but that you will." The ad's focus on *agency* is particularly striking. Recall that for Kierkegaard, despair is born of the misuse and abdication of our agency, as we veer toward possibility or necessity. Celebrity Cruises promises to remove agency from the equation altogether. It seemingly resolves the despair that one can feel in the face of endless possibility by conjuring up and actualizing a dream-like possibility that eliminates the threat of error.

This sounds appealing, but what it means is that the self is relinquishing a fundamental capacity required for full selfhood: the work required to authentically choose among various existential possibilities – the capacity to imagine and exercise choices, make possible errors, and incur ensuing regrets and dissatisfaction. Surrendering the need to grapple with possibility, we are left with an engineered necessity to which we all-too quickly accede. Even though it is an aesthetically charged and pleasant necessity (in this case, a pleasure cruise), it ultimately, as Kierkegaard so perceptively warns, morphs into the despair of necessity. It is a version of Odysseus' plight with the goddess Calypso in Homer's *Odyssey*. Odysseus' dream of getting to sleep with a goddess becomes a reality, but it soon becomes cause for despair, as Odysseus is trapped within this prison of pleasure. The leisure cruise offers a reprieve from the agency and strain required by work (the despair of necessity that often accompanies work), but in the end, it trades one necessity for another.

Ultimately, the escape offered by the cruise, like Odysseus' fate with Calypso, will disappoint. Despair may remain dormant or unconscious for a time, but it will surface. This "idealized" necessity will eventually be exposed. Wallace charts this trajectory within himself. At the outset of his week-long cruise, Wallace notices with sympathy the countless and often unseen laborers who attend to and anticipate each passenger's every need. The leisure the cruise offers requires the work of an extensive servant class. Initially, Wallace's gaze catalogs the humanity of the menial staff, while also noting his own discomfort at being constantly served. There is, however, a shift in his consciousness – an emerging sense of entitlement. Whereas before he was delighted and overwhelmed that room service would clean his room multiple times a day, he eventually comes to expect it, becoming slightly chafed when they run a bit behind schedule. This impatience also creeps into his dining experience, where he comes to expect a waiter to arrive within minutes. Rather than satiation, Wallace discovers what he describes as the "ur-American" part of himself "that craves pampering and passive pleasure: the dissatisfied-infant part of me, the part that always and indiscriminately WANTS." (1996, p. 51). This part, Wallace well notes, "by its very nature and essence," is insatiable (p. 51). In response to gratification, it simply adjusts "its desires upward until it once again levels out at its homeostasis of terrible dissatisfaction" (p. 51). The necessities, however ideal, ultimately will fail to satisfy. This fact is made more acute when his cruise ship, the *Nadir*, docks next to another cruise ship, the *Dreamward*. To Wallace the *Dreamward*, by comparison, appeared sleeker, brighter, and a more perfect shade of white, in contrast to the *Nadir's* cream, buff color.

Eventually, as expected, Wallace experiences the ultimate "falsehood at the dark heart of Celebrity's brochure" (p. 51). This is the lie that this experience will satisfy the part of us that "always and only WANTS ..." (p. 51). The cruise industry is effective (as is the contemporary leisure writ large) at perpetuating this myth because we *want to believe* that "this ultimate fantasy vacation will be enough pampering, that this time the luxury and pleasure will be so completely and faultlessly administered that my infantile part will be sated at last" (p. 52).

The use of the word *pamper* is striking. As the ad promises, cruise attendees will get to do what they have not done in a long time: "Absolutely Nothing." The culmination of total relaxation is getting to do absolutely nothing, while experiencing "stressless indulgence."

This almost sounds quasi-contemplative, as one enters into a state of complete oblivion. Pondering this promise, Wallace poignantly asks, "'How long has it been since you did Absolutely Nothing?'" How long, Wallace asks, has it been since you had "every need met *choicelessly* from someplace outside me, without having to ask ...'"? [my emphasis] (p. 37). During that time, Wallace notes, we were also floating, and we were probably "dreadless" and "... having a really good time ...." Celebrity Cruises seeks to replicate the experience of being a fetus in utero, returning us to an infantile state of warmth, pleasure, and partial consciousness (p. 37). Rather than restore the self, which requires synthesizing possibility and necessity, the leisure Celebrity Cruises anaesthetizes the self.

For very similar reasons, it is understandable why drugs are so incredibly appealing and addictive, offering, as they do, a much swifter path to the same end promised by Celebrity Cruises: the relaxed and ultimately anaesthetized self. Renton, a heroin addict and the major protagonist of the film *Trainspotting* powerfully captures the dynamics at work:

> Choose life. Choose a job. Choose a career. Choose a family, Choose a fucking big television, Choose washing machines, cars .... choose dental insurance. Choose fixed-interest mortgage repayments. Choose a starter home. Choose your friends. I chose not to choose life: I chose something else. And the reasons? There are no reasons. Who needs reasons when you've got heroin? People think it's all about misery and desperation and death and all that shite, which is not to be ignored, but what they forget is the pleasure of it. Otherwise, we wouldn't do it. After all, we're not fucking stupid. At least, we're not that fucking stupid. Take the best orgasm you ever had, multiply it by a thousand and you're still nowhere near it. (Hodge, 1996)

Renton's musings illuminate, in stark fashion, the aesthetic disposition – a release from having to choose – a release from agency altogether. In choosing not to choose life, and in choosing heroin, Renton is essentially not making a choice, surrendering his agency altogether. His marginal selfhood wills to escape into a state of oblivion.

Underneath this desire for pleasure and escape, Wallace discerns a desire to give ourselves away. In an interview, he shares this revealing insight:

> The root of [the word] addict in Latin is the word *addicere*, which means religious devotion. It was an attribute of beginning monks. There is an element in the book [*Infinite Jest*] in which various people are living out something that I think is true, which is that we all worship. We all have a religious impulse. We can choose, to an extent, what we worship, but the myth that we worship nothing and give ourselves away to nothing, simply sets ourselves up to give ourselves away to something different. For instance, pleasure or drugs or the idea of having a lot of money, being able to buy nice stuff. (2003)

Amusement leisure is a form of worship – a desire to give ourselves away which, at its best, can actually empower our sense of self. However, amusement leisure activities are often marked by a desire to escape the self, to check out, or to "veg out." In "vegging out," we are seeking a reprieve from the demands of daily existence (especially the toil of work and other duties) and anxiety about our agency. The expression "vegging out" is revealing in itself. Deriving from the medical, "vegetive state," to "veg out" literally means to be numb to the world.

While I think Wallace's account of amusement is on to something, as he insightfully reveals the dynamics in play, it is bleak. Cruises and contemporary leisure appear to be hopelessly shallow and empty diversions. Accordingly, consumers of this kind of amusement appear to be pacified zombies, with Wallace positioning himself as the profound intellectual-journalist who sees through this ocean of shallowness. Yet, the problematic dynamics he reveals – especially the anaesthetizing pacification that contemporary amusement aims to seduce us into – play out differently within the minds and hearts of each individual. Even within the midst of a cruise event, there are possibilities for meaningful leisure. Certainly, on Wallace's cruise, there probably were practitioners of genuine leisure, but his preoccupation with the dynamics of amusement leisure keeps this hidden from view.

Most of us, given social commitments, and the relentless saturation of amusement culture, have to participate, to some degree, in cruise-like activities. The question is how we might resist the negative propensities that amusement culture draws us into. Recall that the self requires a synthesis of possibility and necessity, lest it fall into despair and suffer existential boredom. Contemporary leisure, often unwittingly, neglects this dynamic and synthesis. Leisure is a break from the strain of work – a slackening of our agency. Our instinct for leisure, for addiction, for worship, is understandable, but it can easily tend toward an abdication of agency. We can become stuck within a work–amusement quagmire, with work straining and taxing our agency and leisure slacking and relaxing it.

There is, though, an alternative to the work–leisure treadmill. The instinct to pursue leisure is on to something important, but the forms and methods we have developed for attending to this desire are, when looked at more closely, indeed peculiar. It is the classical tradition of leisure that provides better resources for obtaining the good that popular and industrial leisure aims for, without the self-anaesthetization that is characteristic of contemporary leisure.

Aristotle on Leisure

At this point, Aristotle's discussion of leisure in the *Nicomachean Ethics* is especially pertinent to this matter. Nature itself, Aristotle contends, requires that we are "capable of being at leisure in noble fashion" (2013, p. 225). Again, our instincts, Aristotle suggests, point to leisure as an essential part of human existence. Burdened by work, and distracted by amusement, Aristotle observes that we often do not know what true leisure is, nor how to pursue and enjoy it. Instead, we tend to confuse amusement with leisure – a conflation that is far more common today than in Aristotle's time. Amusement, Aristotle says, is a "sort of relaxation, which we need because we cannot work continuously" (2013, p. 193). It is a necessary break from work that enables greater productivity. It is especially despots, notes Aristotle, who confuse leisure and amusement, which is not surprising given that they are disordered, unvirtuous souls, who follow the whims of their undisciplined passions. Their judgment, Aristotle says, cannot be trusted. They are like children who foolishly assume amusement to be the supreme end of activity. To underscore this point, Aristotle says how ridiculous it is to claim that we suffer, go to war, and defend our nation all for the sake of amusement.

Amusement, in Aristotle's account, occupies the same place that leisure does in our current context. It is a relaxing break from work, since we cannot work continuously. Yet we should, Aristotle cautions, introduce amusements "only at suitable times, and they should be our medicines, for the emotion which they create in the soul is relaxation ..." (2013, p. 193). Relaxation, we have seen, is the supreme *telos* or purpose that Celebrity Cruises offers. Yet far from our ultimate telos, Aristotle advises that amusement should be treated like a medicine that we administer with care. Medicine is a means or is instrumental for assisting or restoring work productivity, good health, or flourishing. It is not itself, however, constitutive of good health, any more than a recovered tuberculosis sufferer should continue taking doses of antibiotics.

While amusement is subsumed under work, as a mere respite, Aristotle places leisure as the end or purpose of work. "We work, in order to be at leisure." Recall that the modern definition of leisure is referenced only in negative relationship to work: Leisure is simply that which is not work. This suggests that our ultimate meaning and purpose are derived from working. In Aristotle's account, by contrast, work is simply defined as that which is "un-leisurely." Leisure, not work, Aristotle contends is our ultimate purpose. Our instinct for leisure, Aristotle says, is not only in accord with our nature, but aligns with what he describes as our highest nature. Leisure's significance and importance transcends both the world of work and politics, for both spheres are strictly a means toward the greater end of leisure. This telos or summons to a higher life of leisure Aristotle goes on to say, somewhat mysteriously, is "too high for" human beings. It "is not insofar as he is man that he will live so, but insofar as something divine is present in him ..." (2013, p. 193). Lofty as this superhuman goal may be, Aristotle insists that we must strive for leisure, aiming "to live in accordance with the best thing in us; for even if it be small in bulk, much more does it in power and worth surpass everything" (2013, p. 193). This longing for leisure, Aristotle goes on to say, is "the authoritative and better part" of a human being (p. 193).

As the telos or supreme good of human flourishing, then, leisure for Aristotle redirects the meaning and significance of all other activities, including work, politics, and amusement. They are or should be understood and practiced as means toward securing leisure. Given that, in this framework, the entire endeavors of work and politics are relativized by leisure, what though does Aristotle actually mean by leisure? Considering human beings, Aristotle notes that reason, or the intellect, is our supreme faculty. But the activity of the human intellect, he observes, is not simply employed for technical or pragmatic purposes but is intrinsically worthwhile. Human beings, Aristotle says, "desire to know." They *intrinsically* enjoy wondering, learning, and figuring things out, apart from the utility that such activities may yield. More than free time, or the absence of practical necessities, leisure is a state of mind that simply enjoys the act of knowing.

Thinking with and extending Aristotle, 1,500 years later, St. Thomas Aquinas (1225–1274) notes two distinct capacities that inform our quest to know and understand, which he describes as *ratio* and *intellectus*. The Aquinas scholar and philosopher Josef Pieper (1904–1997) illuminates this distinction,

> Ratio is the power of discursive thought, of searching and re-searching, abstracting, refining, and concluding [cf. Latin dis-currere, "to run to and fro"], whereas intellectus refers to the ability of "simply looking" (simplex intuitus), to which the truth presents itself as a landscape presents itself to the eye. (1998, p. 32)

This key distinction, notes Pieper, was dealt a fatal blow by Immanuel Kant (1724–1804), the preeminent philosophical figure of the Western Enlightenment. For Kant, the human act of knowing is exclusively discursive: a busy, active capacity that sizes up, compares, abstracts, proves, and investigates to produce knowledge. Intellectus is no longer in the picture, only ratio. Knowing is thus regarded exclusively as an active mental effort.

This is a significant point. The crux of the leisure tradition from Aristotle to Benedict to Aquinas up to the present depends on this key distinction, which Kant and his successors discarded. Human knowing, Pieper asserts, is a mutual interplay of ratio and intellectus; whoever can recognize an element of intellectual vision within discursive reasoning; whoever, finally, can retain in philosophy an element of contemplation of being as a whole such a person will have to grant that a characterization of knowing and philosophy as "work" is not only not exhaustive, but does not even reach the core of the matter, and that something essential is in fact missing from such a definition. (1998, p. 33)

For Pieper – and for Aristotle and Aquinas before him – intellectus is our intuitive faculty; ratio is our discursive faculty – it is the ego applying itself to understand and make sense of the world. Ratio is a tool we employ for analytical purposes. Intellectus, however, is a disposition of the mind to receive a gift. With ratio, the self achieves understanding; with intellectus, the self receives illumination. This recalls the connection between worship and leisure that Wallace notes. Simone Weil describes the intellectus movement this way: "May I disappear in order that those things that I see may become perfect in their beauty from the very fact that they are no longer things that I see" (1997, p. 89).

The modern Jewish theologian Abraham Heschel (1907–1972) makes a similar distinction between reason and wonder, with reason correlating to ratio and wonder to intellectus. "Through the first," Heschel explains, "we try to explain or to adapt the world to our concepts, through the second we seek to adapt our minds to the world" (1977, p. 21). Heschel further illuminates the distinction:

[In wonder] the person meets the world, not with the tools they have made but with the soul with which they were born;… [the world] is not an object, a thing that is given to the senses, but a state of fellowship that embraces her or him and all things; not a particular fact but the startling situation that there are facts at all; being; the presence of a universe; the unfolding of time. (1977, p. 38)

The leisure tradition, then, upholds a vision of the human being as both active and contemplative. While ratio is born of work and striving, intellectus is not work or achievement; it is a gift. This conception is challenging to modern ears because, as Pieper notes, we valorize effort, distrusting anything that comes easily. We mistrust "everything that is effortless" and "can only enjoy with a good conscience" what we have "acquired with toil and trouble" (Pieper, 1998, p. 39).

The contemporary French Catholic philosopher and theologian Jean Luc-Marion (1947–) sheds further light on what an intellectus approach to beholding consists of, describing it as an ability to recognize that certain phenomena are saturated, which is to say, they exceed our human conceptual schemes. Ratio aims to bring phenomena within the purview of our conceptual schemes. This move, or attempt to distill and "simplify [phenomena] for us," Marion notes, risks masking "their exuberant splendor" (p. 20). Rather than "an object or being," saturated phenomena are better understood as a given feature of the world, which emit an excess of intuitions that exceed our cognitive structures and conceptual frames (2002, p. 20). Such phenomena, Marion contends, "possess a priori an infinity of meanings that cannot be captured by us once and for all, but that demand that we relate to them receptively and that we develop our understanding of them in a form of endless hermeneutics" (Henrickson, 2013, p. 746). There is, in the encounter with a saturated phenomenon, a sense "that they contain something more, or are richer, than we grasp by means of our understanding" (Henrickson, 2013, p. 746).

From this perspective, therefore, intellectus is what enables and sustains leisure, disposing a contemplative and humble engagement with the world. It is the seat of leisure. The intellectus faculty is not simply a matter of receiving sense data or information from our environment; rather, it is a mode of reception or special kind of openness that, in turn, can lead to dramatic moments of insight and epiphany. The young Dutch Jewish writer and Holocaust victim Etty Hillesum (1914–1943) illuminates this interior movement, as she moves from a ratio to an intellectus approach to beholding. She describes her experience as follows:

> And here I have hit upon something essential. [In the past] whenever I saw a beautiful flower, what I longed to do with it was press it to my heart, or eat it all up. It was more difficult with a piece of beautiful scenery, but the feeling was the same. I was too sensual, I might also write too greedy.

> I yearned physically for all I thought was beautiful, wanted to own it. Hence that painful longing that could never be satisfied, the pining for something I thought unattainable. (1981, p. 10)

Eventually a change occurs inside of her – a change she could not fully account for. She describes a walk outside as follows:

> It was dusk, soft hues in the sky, mysterious silhouettes of houses, trees alive with the light through the tracery of their branches, in short, enchanting. And then I knew precisely how I had felt in the past. Then all the beauty would have gone like a stab to my heart and I would not have known what to do with the pain. Then I would have felt the need to write, to compose verses, but the words would still have refused to come. I would have felt utterly miserable, wallowed in the pain and exhausted myself as a result. The experience would have sapped all my energy. Now I know it for what it was: mental masturbation.... But that night ... I reacted quite differently.... I was just as deeply moved by that mysterious, still landscape in the dusk as I might have been before, but somehow I no longer wanted to own it. I went home invigorated and got to work. And the scenery stayed with me, in the background, as a cloak about my soul, to put it poetically for once, but no longer held me back: I no longer "masturbated" with it. (1981, p. 11)

Breaking from her possessive, grasping approach, Hillesum was able to experience a vision of intellectus. She was able to delight in things as they are, without a desire to own or exploit them. As Hillesum suggests, ratio, which seems to serve our autonomous grasping self, is often prompted by our compulsive self – the restless, acquisitive, controlling, the ur-American self that Wallace recounts.

More than simply time apart, then, leisure is a state of inner tranquility that enables the soul to greet the world receptively, in awareness of its mystery, rather than as something to be mastered. This mysterious encounter is negative but also positive. It is negative in the sense that the person senses there is something more to know, something they cannot grasp – "the sense that the world is a deeper, wider, more mysterious thing than appeared to the day-to-day understanding" (Pieper, 1998, p. 105), It is positive in the sense that the experience of leisure is inspired by a hope that sets one on a journey. Wonder causes one to pause and ponder over the mystery of being. Heschel elaborates: "... while the ineffable is a term of negation indicating limitation of expression, its content is intensely affirmative, denoting an allusiveness to something meaningful, for which we possess no means of expression" (Heschel, 1977, p. 22). Leisure, Pieper elaborates, "lives on affirmation. It is not the same as the absence of activity ... or even as an inner quiet. It is rather like the stillness in the conversation of lovers, which is fed by their oneness" (1998, p. 52).

A person capable of genuine leisure, notes Pieper, is not in need of constant new and different or sensationalized experiences. Such a need is a sure sign that one has lost the capacity for leisure. Boredom, Pieper contends, is evidence such a person has lost "the spiritual power to be leisurely" (1998, p. 73). Rather than being capable of wonder or being astonished, our vision can become jaded in both senses of this word: "fatigued by work" and "dull, apathetic, or cynical by experience or by having or seeing too much of something" (Merriam-Webster, 2021). Rather than seeing too much, Marion rightly suggests that the problem is that we stop seeing enough; we take things for granted, as fully known and perceived. Leisure or intellectus seeing shakes up our taken-for-granted world. It does not remove one from the things of the world but rather disrupts "the usual meanings, the accustomed evaluations of these things" (Pieper, 1998, p. 117). Marion elaborates:

> The concepts, by which we know what there is to see so well that we no longer take the time or the trouble to go and truly see, serve only to sum them up, simplify them for us, so as to mask their exuberant splendor. Most of the time, we want to get an idea of things without having any intention of seeing them, so that we can handle them easily, like equipment. If we were to forget their concepts, we would see that there are so many things to see—so many things to see in this old violin on the simple stool, a rumpled newspaper and sad little vase. The cubist painter knows this, he who no longer wants to bring into visibility what just anyone—forewarned, busy, practical-minded—sees. (2002, p. 217)

Ratio, in contrast to the attentiveness Marion calls forth, tends to be our impatient default setting. What Pieper and Hillesum both highlight is that the practice of leisure establishes agency in a different way. Where ratio agency is active and grasping; intellectus agency is receptive, humble, and attentive. Recall that contemporary versions of leisure (better understood as amusement) aim to relinquish agency. Classical leisure seeks to restore a form of agency that is eclipsed by chronic busyness and the constant itch to be doing or achieving something.

But contrary to what might be expected, the receptivity that intellectus involves does not come easily. Because this leisured condition is less at one's disposal (as opposed to ratio, which offers an illusory control, but is in fact often more driven than directed) – there is something gifted about it, as experiences of awe and wonder suggest – it is, paradoxically, more difficult to attain. It takes work not to work – as perhaps a workaholic might attest. Ideally, over a span of time, there should be a balance between the intellectus and ratio. The world of work, however, not only limits the time for leisure but also more significantly impoverishes our imagination so that we are not able to envision something beyond the work–amusement treadmill. To the extent that genuine leisure is a possibility, it is fleeting because we lack the tools and discipline it requires.

Leisure is fragile; it is easily overshadowed and displaced by practical concerns. It requires, as the British philosopher Michael Oakeshott (1901–1990) observed, a concerted effort to, "disentangle oneself from the here and now of current happenings and engagements, to detach oneself from the urgencies of the local and the contemporary, to explore and enjoy a release from having to consider things in terms of their contingent features ..." (Oakeshott 1989, pp. 30–31). Rather than passivity, leisure involves an intense practice of self-examination that cultivates true freedom by guarding against idleness, compulsive busyness, and pointless desires.

This transformative leisure that Aristotle and others cited here illuminate is increasingly harder to secure. The accounts of leisurely experience considered thus far, however, help us first to see or envision what a richer conception of leisure might be in contrast to the agency-relinquishing of amusement leisure that prevails today. Leisure in its most compelling sense is a form of experience in which we are (1) *attentive*, as we encounter a saturated phenomenon;

(2) *receptive* as we engage our intellectus faculty while resisting the pull of our busy *ratio* faculty; and (3) ultimately, *transformative* as ratio gives way to intellectus beholding. This transformation is ordinarily gradual and subtle. There may be epiphanies of leisurely beholding, as Hillesum reveals, but these will be fleeting unless they are situated within a nurturing context.

Leisure is a new way of being, which confers a new way of seeing. The process begins with receptivity, first disposing the self to receive a gift. While seemingly passive, receptivity requires careful preparation, especially removing the clutter – especially the mental, physical, and cultural that typically surrounds us. As St. Augustine (354–430) observed, we are often presented with "good things to us, but our hands are too full to receive them."[3] Receptivity involves emptying our hands and minds so that we can receive something new. This move must then be followed by a vigilant attempt to fend off and still our busy minds, which are prone to flit from one thing to the next. The Dutch theologian Henri Nouwen (1932–1996) illuminates what this struggle looks like within the context of prayer:

> When we sit down for half an hour—without talking to someone, listening to music, watching television or reading a book—and try to become very still, we often find ourselves so overwhelmed by our noisy inner voices that we can hardly wait to get busy and distracted again. Our inner life often looks like a banana tree full of jumping monkeys! But when we decide not to run away and stay focused, these monkeys may gradually go away because of lack of attention. (2000, p. 20)

Overcoming this struggle in his own experience, Nouwen began to experience a transformed self, while dying to an old self. The boredom avoidance treadmill is a familiar and well-trodden path. Yet like prisoners in Plato's cave, even while recognizing despair for what it is, we nevertheless cling to this existence, as it becomes a familiar, albeit bleak, comfort zone. Our boredom avoidance practices, more than things we do, are who we are. They are hardened ways of coping with this unpleasant fact of existence. Becoming a

---

[3] As quoted from Gerald May's *Addiction and Grace* (2007, p. 17).

person of leisure requires that we first diagnose our condition and then pursue an alternative set of practices and/or an alternative way of engaging with current practices.

Conclusion

Boredom avoidance is a way of being. The classical tradition proposes a different way of being that ameliorates the despair that afflicts the bored self. Each disposition or mental outlook (boredom avoidance and contemplative leisure) encompasses a different set of habits, which shape and form a different self. While leisure is, as Aristotle notes, our greatest good and the fulfillment of our nature, it does not come easily.

Leisure is fundamentally a way of living. We cannot think or argue our way into a new way of living. Rather, we must live our way into a new way of thinking. In this respect, leisure, as an art, requires the acquisition of virtues (states of a well-ordered soul) in order for it to come into existence. While we may, on occasion, experience moments of leisure, the leisurely disposition (as an enduring state) does not emerge by accident; it requires discipline, practice, and constant repetition.

We have a clearer sense of the inner state of a soul at leisure. But how do we get there? What kinds of activities or practices come to our assistance? To acquire a virtue, Aristotle says we must repeatedly perform virtuous actions again and again, so that they become an ingrained, fixed part of our character. Likewise, in order to develop the spiritual capacity to become leisurely, we must practice leisure. Yet, because it is primarily a state of beholding, leisure is not exclusive to any one discrete art or practice. It can be embodied within a variety of activities. There are, though, distinctive features or qualities of leisurely practice that can be nurtured. In Chapter 5, I explore and examine these characteristics that provide context and direction for how to cultivate the art of leisure.

5 THE ART OF LEISURE

Leisure promises to offer a compelling response to the widespread malaise of boredom and despair. Rather than being a kind of activity that we can book online or buy tickets for, leisure is a state of mind in which we receptively behold the world, attend to its unique sensory and spiritual offerings, and open ourselves to be transformed by the message these have for us. The leisurely state of mind is not to be thought of as a mere respite or break from work, but should imbue our working engagements with meaning, so that our periods of rest are truly restful and restoring. Although this insight, which builds upon Aristotle and Pieper's accounts of leisure, brings us some of the way toward addressing the problem of modern boredom, the question of how can we *enter into* such a leisurely state of mind remains? What kinds of practices, activities, forms of engagement, and rituals can help us learn the art of leisure? This is the central topic of this chapter.

First, I consider Alasdair MacIntyre's neo-Aristotelian notion of "practices." For MacIntyre, practices refer to special forms of human activity that harbor what he calls internal goods, goods to which practitioners progressively gain access as they acquire more experience. Part of what it means to enact a leisurely state of mind is to become attentive to the internal goods of our practical engagements. At the same time, the activities in which we can cultivate and enact leisure should not only be thought of as "practices," in the MacIntyrean sense. Attending only to such practices would narrow the range of human engagement in which leisure can be experienced. More provocative is philosopher Albert

Borgmann's (1937–present) notion of a focal practice, which resonates with MacIntyre's account, but includes a broader range of activities that count as worthwhile practices. While Borgmann's account of focal practices covers what MacIntyre has in mind, it also includes simple activities such as cooking, walking, and reading. Borgmann shows that even and especially in such engagements, we can experience and further cultivate leisure. Drawing from both MacIntyre's and Borgmann's insights, we can discern three tangible ways of cultivating leisure.

On Practices

In order to experience the restoration of genuine leisure, it may appear that we only need to replace time spent on amusement with time dedicated to leisurely pursuits. Instead of a work–amusement cycle, we might envision a work–leisure cycle, with leisure taking the place of amusement. Although this may appear a straightforward measure to fill our lives with more restorative practices, two problems arise when we construe the problem in such a simple way. First, the possibility of an amusement-free life sounds unbearably spartan and drab. The goal, as Aristotle counsels, is not to eliminate amusement but to moderate it. Recall Aristotle's likening amusement to a potent medicine that must be handled with care so we can enjoy its good effects, while steering clear of its harmful extremes, especially addiction. If this is right, then the point of leisure is not to *replace* amusement but to *direct* it – or rather to direct *us* while we engage in it.

Second, and most importantly, fitting leisure within the means–end logic embodied in the "replacement approach" fundamentally misconstrues the nature of leisure itself. Rather than being merely time apart (a weekend) or a specific activity (a vacation), leisure is a condition of the soul – way of engaging with the world that can imbue both our work and our amusements with restorative significance. This understanding, however, requires a different lens through which we see and understand ourselves.

Pieper, in the 1950s, diagnosed in the West an emerging culture of "total work" (Pieper, 1998, p. 43). More than the sheer (and increasing) number of hours of work, Pieper noted a transformation in the way work was viewed. Work (or the necessary tasks of production and consumption) had become the exclusive point of reference for how we see and define ourselves. We are, Pieper feared, increasingly incapable of seeing beyond the working self. The human being (or *Homo sapiens*) has become the human worker (or *Homo faber*). Rather than a robust and rich alternative to work, leisure has been co-opted by work, defined negatively and simply as the absence of work. This shift in vision signifies a change in how we understand the meaning of human existence.

Given how beset we are by utilitarian ways of seeing, we are in danger, the British philosopher and critic Roger Scruton (1944–2020) feared, of "allowing the means to swallow the ends" (Scruton, 2015, p. 26). MacIntyrean practices push against this trend. Rather than primarily extrinsic or utility goods, the "point" of practices is precisely to gain access to the special means of flour- ishing that the activity affords. To ask the question, for example, of someone playing tennis or painting, "what is the point of this practice?" is to miss the heart of the matter. One fails to see that activity is self-justifying or intrinsically worthwhile. So, for another example, the point of gardening considered as a practice is to grow robust plants, in well-tilled healthy soil, in harmony with the natu- ral environment, in community with those who benefit from it, and so forth. If gardening were reduced to "the production of dietary fiber for nutritional purposes," the gardener would lack connec- tion to the intrinsic goods of the practice, focused exclusively on its external goods at the expense of the intrinsic goods that create its authentic value.

Rather than appreciating intrinsic goods, we often become fixated on the extrinsic goods that practices accrue, held captive to a "production-oriented" conception of action (Brewer, 2009, p. 13). To pursue practices rightly, rather than simply as means to some other end, we must prioritize both internal and external goods. Yet often, given our production orientation, we tend to let external goods eclipse the intrinsic goods of a practice. We can see this when children who are pressured by parents, coaches, fans, and a larger cultural ethos to take up extracurricular activities so as to embellish their resumes and win at all costs. Rather than rich activ- ities for physical and cultural expression, such children are condi- tioned to see such activities largely as competitive, prize-winning affairs.[1] By contrast, a positive experience of the intrinsic goods of a sport or hobby provides a young learner a realization of the intrinsic value that they can experience again and again without regard to wins or trophies. While extrinsic goods (prizes, status) are necessarily limited, the goods internal to practices are without limit.

Carol Dweck's work in educational psychology confirms how a focus on extrinsic goods can distort a practice (2006). Children were given a task to perform (drawing with markers). One group was encouraged to take up the task with the promise of receiving prizes (extrinsic goods) for their efforts. For the second group, no rewards were offered, just time allotted for artistic creation. Several weeks later, those who were given prizes were, compared to their peers, less interested in the activity of drawing. The rewardless group, by contrast, showed an enduring interest in the practice of drawing and also produced works of a higher quality.

Philosopher Matthew Crawford, in his book *Shop Class as Soulcraft* (2010), further illumines the distortions that a hyper-focus on extrinsic goods causes. An external reward, Crawford explains, "can affect one's interpretation of one's own motivation, and interpretation that comes to be self-fulfilling" (2010, p. 195). Crawford elaborates:

> A similar effect may account for the familiar fact that when someone turns his hobby into a business, he often loses pleasure in it. Likewise, an intellectual who pursues an academic career gets professionalized, and this may lead him to stop thinking. This line of reasoning suggests that the kind of appreciative attention where one remains focused on what one is doing can arise only in leisure activities. Such a conclusion would put pleasurable absorption beyond the ken of any activity that is undertaken for the sake of making money, because although money is undoubtedly good, it is not intrinsically so. (2010, p. 195)

---

[1] "Dialectical activity" is Brewer's phrasing. It means that certain activities, given the complexity and the level of engagement they require, are constant wellsprings of intrinsic goods.

Crawford's point about interpretation is important to under-score. We can go through the motions of a practice but fail to see, experience, and enjoy its intrinsic goods. The act of leisure, while mediated through certain practices, requires a way of seeing or interpreting experience. Again, leisure is a state of beholding in a certain way. MacIntyre's distinction between intrinsic and extrinsic goods is helpful in suggesting how to move away from a means–end mentality to recognizing and appreciating activities or practices that are intrinsically worthwhile. We cannot, Pieper notes, experience leisure "as long as our interest remains absorbed by the active pursuit of goals, when the 'lens' of our soul is focused on a clearly circumscribed sector, on an objective here and now, on things that are presently 'needed' – and explicitly not on anything else" (1992, p. 7).

Given the intrinsic goods afforded by practices, which include a variety of activities, the pursuit of leisure, we can imag-ine, might simply require working toward excellence in one or more practices. For the bored and restless self, such practices like music-making, writing, sports, are powerful and constructive responses. In addition, pursuing practices successfully involves the acquisition of virtues so as to properly perform and sustain them. Virtues like moderation, patience, and persistence, enable "us to overcome the harms, dangers, temptations and distractions" that disrupt the development of a practice (MacIntyre, 1984, p. 219). So, it seems like the answer to boredom and the pathway into lei-sure, then, is simply to take up a practice or a suite of practices that fill up our available time. To be sure, this is a viable path for some. They find a passion (music, art, writing), and it becomes the center around which they build their lives. It is a constant and productive refuge from boredom – a never-ending wellspring of intrinsic goods.

And yet, three concerns should be noted. The first pertains to the ratio–intellectus distinction. Recall that the intellectus faculty involved in the leisurely state of mind requires a posture of recep-tivity. Developing prowess in a practice, however, requires taking initiative and employing effort, exercising our ratio faculty to make incremental progress. Ever striving toward a more perfect execution of a practice, we can understandably neglect the intellectus move-ment – which involves a mindful recognition and appreciation of the internal goods of a practice as we can currently pursue it. That is, we lay down our striving and enjoy the fact that we get to be a part of an intrinsically worthwhile endeavor with like-minded individuals. Losing the capacity for this kind of enjoyment is a common experience for musicians and athletes who, straining for perfection, often lament that they no longer enjoy their craft. The loss of fun is a sure sign that ratio drudgery has eclipsed intellectus enjoyment.

A second related concern is the touch of exclusivity that seems to color the MacIntyrean conception of practice. While the range of what MacIntyre considers to be a genuine practice is broad, it nevertheless is a select group of activities. Consider, for example, MacIntyre's definition of a practice:

> By a practice I am going to mean any coherent and complex form of socially established cooperative human activity through which goods internal to that form of activity are realized in the course of trying to achieve those standards of excellence which are appropriate to, and partially definitive of, that form of activity, with the result that human powers to achieve excellence, and human conceptions of the ends and goods involved, are systematically extended. (1984, p. 175)

According to MacIntyre, there needs to be a sufficient degree of complexity for an activity to count as a practice, and practitioners must acquire a certain level of proficiency in order to be able to experience intrinsic goods. Brewer, extending MacIntyre's line of thinking, describes such practices as having a "dialectical" quality to them. As "dialectical activities," they "can be reiterated indefinitely, with each successive engagement yielding a clearer grasp of the activity's proper form and preparing the way for a still more adequate and hence more revealing engagement in it" (Brewer, 2009, p. 37). Practices, Brewer explains, have a "self-unveiling character, in the sense that each successive engagement yields a further stretch of understanding of the goods internal to the activity, hence of what would count as a proper engagement in it" (p. 37).

MacIntyre notes several specific examples of practices, including painting, sports, and scientific inquiry, among others. Tic-tac-toe, he notes, is not a practice, nor is the specific skill of throwing a football or laying bricks. Leisure, then, viewed as accessing the intrinsic value of practices, is simply not available to the novice. Intuitively, this may sound reasonable, given that novices certainly cannot fully appreciate the practices that they are growing accustomed to. However, from another perspective, the exclusivity suggested here is deeply problematic, suggesting that genuine leisure is only available to the accomplished virtuoso, athlete, or craftsperson.

While leisure is certainly an art that requires discipline, it is an art of a different order. Leisure is a practice that is available to everyone, including the gifted and not-so-gifted. The talented – those with a capacity to achieve practical excellence – are vulnerable to misconstruing leisure as yet another domain where they can achieve and accomplish. This mindset works against the receptive intellectus. Recall the receptivity that intellectus involves. Rather *than a gift we obtain, leisure is a gift we receive*. This is the fundamental movement to be cultivated.

A third challenge pertains to what novelist Walker Percy (1916–1990) describes as the problem of reentry. An experience of the internal goods of a practice is often followed by a letdown when our practical engagement with it is over. By contrast, the mundane, ordinary tasks of life are experienced as even more drab than usual, relative to the intrinsic goods of MacIntyrean practices. Percy asks, "what did William Faulkner do after writing the last sentence of *Light in August?*" What did "Dostoevsky do after finishing *The Idiot?*" (2011, p. 142). The answer is Faulkner got drunk for a week, and Dostoevsky spent three days and nights at a roulette table. Reentry into ordinary life is difficult, given the sharp contrast with intoxicating artistic or imaginative creation. Einstein captures this tension well:

> One of the strongest motives that lead men to art and science is escape from everyday life with its painful crudity and hopeless dreariness, from the fetters of one's own ever-shifting desires. A finely tempered nature longs to escape from the personal life into the world of objective perception and thought. (Einstein and Pyenson, 2006, p. 43)

The dilemma applies even to the connoisseurs of art as well as its creators. What, Percy asks, does the reader or moviegoer do when the book or movie ends? "How long does his exaltation last?" (Percy, 2011, p. 142). Rather than renewing us to attend to the demands of life, practices can set us up for a letdown, and as in the cases of Dostoevsky and Faulkner, lead to a propensity to turn toward anaesthetizing amusement for escape.

Thus, while MacIntyre's notion of internal goods illuminates a core constituent of leisurely engagement, the demands that MacIntyrean practices place upon the subject to exercise intense ratio thinking militate against a genuinely leisurely mindset. In addition, the pursuit of excelling in a practice can take over, with a creeping perfectionism that prompts more restive striving than restful appreciation. Finally, the problem of reentry can actually set the individual up to grasp for amusement over leisure when the joys of a practice let up. Is there a conception of leisurely practice that can attend to these various problems?

On Focal Practices

Our answer lies in Borgmann's notion of a focal practice, which complements and refines a MacIntyrean definition of practices in the art of leisure. By focal, Borgmann is not referring to the modern technical definition to describe optics or points of convergence in geometry, but to its more ancient denotation. Deriving from the Latin, focus literally means "domestic hearth" or "fireplace." The hearth, prior to the development of ventilation heating systems, was the figurative and literal center of the home. Thus, for Borgmann, focal practices are unique in that they – like the hearth – structure and direct attention, engaging us with the things that constitute them. It is the *quality of attention* (where it is directed and how it is directed) that focal practices require that is meaningful and salutary. A focal practice trains and guides us to attend deeply, in a sustained way, to one thing, overcoming the temptation to move from one thing to the next. In so doing, a focal practice "gathers the relations of its context and radiates into its surroundings and informs them" (Borgmann, 1987, p. 197). Focal practices change the way we see and interpret, to the extent that we give ourselves over to them.

Among examples of focal practices, Borgmann includes cooking and walking. These are practices that engage both our bodies and minds and connect us with others. We can certainly cook or walk alone, but doing so for or with others extends the intrinsic goods of the practice. Focal opportunities surround us but only come into full view when we faithfully engage with a focal practice. The daily starting and tending of a fire, for example, can be a focal practice, and the ax, the wood, and the furnace are the focal things with which this practice is engaged. Similarly, cooking is a focal practice, which engages with focal things like a cutting knife, leaves, a cut of meat, etc. The focal practice of running or walking engages us with several focal things – the sky, the air, and perhaps a forest. A focal practice enables the *seeing and appreciating of* a focal thing in its uniqueness – a violin, an earthenware jug, a running trail, and a tattered old book.

Consider the significance of the focal practices of running and cooking as Borgmann illuminate them:

> Running and the culture of the table are such focal things and practices. We have all been touched by them in one way or another. If we have not participated in a vigorous or competitive run, we have certainly taken walks; we have felt with surprise, perhaps, the pleasure of touching the earth, of feeling the wind, smelling the rain, of having the blood course through our bodies more steadily. In the preparation of a meal we have enjoyed the simple tasks of washing leaves and cutting bread; we have felt the force and generosity of being served a good wine and home-made bread. Such experiences have been particularly vivid when we came upon them after much sitting and watching indoors, after a surfeit of readily available snacks and drinks. To encounter a few simple things was liberating and invigorating. The normal clutter and distraction fall away.... (1987, p. 200)

What is valuable about Borgmann's account of these practices is his framing of them so as to encourage intellectus beholding, as a counterbalance to the more ratio-focused pursuit of excellence that MacIntyre describes. For example, instead of discussing how the novice runner moves into greater connection with the internal goods of the "practice of running," as she gains more experience, Borgmann highlights simple, more accessible aspects of the running and walking experience to which each person can connect and relate no matter their level of accomplishment. Borgmann mentions the pleasure of "touching the earth" and "feeling the wind." These focal things are so simple and seemingly banal that they can easily be overlooked, passed off as irrelevant and even distracting from the (external) goals before us. And yet when we are within a focal practice – which is to say, when we are running or walking or cooking such that we are *sensitized to their focusing power* – we see and feel these things anew, as if we had discovered them for the very first time.

Borgmann's conception of practices and the examples he offers – though sketched only briefly here – offers not only a promising way into the leisurely state of mind; it additionally addresses the three concerns raised about MacIntyre's practices. Walking and cooking, for example, two of the core focal practices Borgmann considers, do not require technical expertise – at least in their common forms. Rather, each simply demands a basic level of attention and commitment to experience both their intrinsic and extrinsic goods. Moreover, the sheer ordinariness of these activities makes them widely available to amateurs and experts alike. While cooking can certainly be susceptible to a perfectionist bent, the mere fact that it needs to be done everyday mitigates against this tendency. Percy's problem regarding the difficult reentry to ordinary life from high forms of intellectual or aesthetic activity is also addressed by Borgmann's practices. Rather than specialized activities set apart, cooking and walking are part of the mundane fabric of everyday life. In these ordinary practices, there are possibilities for leisurely attentiveness that often go unnoticed and unrealized. If we can harbor them, then the problem of crossing in and out of an engagement threshold is dissolved.

Borgmann's emphasis on focal things is as much about the particular way of seeing things, as it is about the things in themselves. We might have a fleeting moment of appreciation for an old tree or oak table, but it is only when we commit to a focal practice with integrity and consistency that we are able to see and appreciate, even savor, focal things with the consistency requisite for them to have a meaningful impact on our lives. This way of seeing, and hence of engaging the attentive intellectus, is born of commitment to a focal practice.

The problem is that the contemporary world seems to be waging war on precisely our capacity to make such commitments.

The price of technological convenience, Borgmann notes, comes at the expense of focal practices and things. Instead of cooking, we eat out or microwave prepackaged food. Instead of going for a walk, we stare at screens to unwind. Rather than seeking meaningful things to see and attend to, we are surrounded by generic, mass-produced things. Pitchers, cups, books, shoes, and homes are simply facsimiles – replicates of an original. The problem with this phenomenon (in addition to the waste of resources) is that things lose their singularity. Given this, there is no reason to grant them our singular attention. Objects recede into the background. The tools we use (our keyboard, plastic cups, a disposable pen, a razor) are hardly noticeable, except when they malfunction, in which case they are promptly replaced. Rather than see, appreciate, and experience things, we are conditioned to use them and be done with them. What is at stake is how we are thus conditioned to see and engage with our world.

Imagine a single plastic Sprite bottle amidst a hundred of them stacked on a soda aisle. Apart from its bright green color, there is little that captures our attention, and nothing really worth seeing. It is situated within a cacophony of colors and shapes on the shelves all aimed at arresting our attention. Bombarded daily with such advertising, we become conditioned to tune out the relentless attempts to divert and direct our attention. Yet, the remarkable success of advertising and social media indicates how easily we are co-opted. If not the Sprite ad, some other craftier ad will draw us in.

Adept at this game, the contemporary commercial news media tends more toward the voyeuristic than the informative – each day or hour offering a new cycle of clickbait. This process both catches and corrodes attention. The personalized algorithms (based on our search histories and other tracking mechanisms) are ingenious at keeping, directing, and holding our attention, while at the same time limiting our capacity for deep attention or the kind of attention required in order for a focal practice to get off the ground. Sociologist Zygmunt Bauman (1925–2017) illuminates how modern consumerism works its spell on our consciousness, both gripping and weakening our faculty of attention:

> Consumed goods should bring satisfaction immediately, requiring no learning of skills and no lengthy groundwork,

but the satisfaction should end the moment the time needed for consumption is up, and that time ought to be reduced to bare minimum. The needed reduction is best achieved if the consumers cannot hold their attention nor focus their desire on any object for long; if they are impatient, impetuous, and restive; and above all if they are easily excitable and predisposed to quickly lose interest. (2005, p. 37)

Focal practices, and the things they direct us to carefully engage with, stand in direct opposition to this dynamic. This is why they are promising terrain for understanding the practice and art of leisure. What Bauman et al. reveal, though, is how truly unleisured our world is, keeping us in a state of perpetual impatience.

Recall that the bored self struggles with finding something worthwhile to attend to. Focal practices address this angst. Yet to the bored self, such practices appear too mundane and too drab to be a cure; instead, the bored self is conditioned to respond to the brightest, loudest, and most shocking volley for its attention. Yet to sustain this constant stimulation, each arresting moment needs to be surpassed by yet another and another. In an alarming paradox, we become bored by this very stimulation. What promises to be yet another exciting, stimulating distraction turns out to simply be more of the same.

The challenge, thus, is not necessarily to seek out "special" forms of activity that promise to redeem us from our boredom once and for all. This is, again, a downside of attending only to MacIntyrean practices. In our pursuit of such engagements, we might be acting on the same stimulation-hungry mindset that is the very source of our problems. Instead, the problem before us is, at once, more demanding and more simple. Our task is to find out how to see the possibilities laden within everyday focal practices and enact them in an especially attentive and reflective way, in spite of the forces impinging upon us to ignore their value and significance. How, then, might we usher in such a transformation of view? How should we begin to practice the art of leisure?

Directives for Leisure

In what follows I offer three directives for cultivating the art of leisure: *becoming an apprentice, cultivating a spirit of study,* and *contemplating or remembering our epiphanies.* By apprenticeship, I am referring to submitting to the wisdom of a tradition and elders who have sustained it to ensure fidelity and accountability to focal practices, as well as guidance on how to perform focal practices in the right way. Study refers to cultivating disciplined attention for intellectus beholding, resisting mere restive curiosity and a culture of spectacle. The contemplation of epiphanies involves funding the imagination with specific stories and vignettes that illuminate the ideal we are striving for.

To understand the need for apprenticeship, we must recall the goods internal to a practice. In the early stages of learning a language or instrument, intrinsic goods are a distant if not a faint possibility. Even our conception of those goods, as a novice, is illusory and often does not match how we will eventually come to experience and understand the nature of the goods internal to the practice. Only proficient practitioners have this insider knowledge, born of experience, and developing expertise. Although, as noted, the attention to experience and expertise can introduce a problematic exclusivity into the domain of leisurely practices, there is plainly a need for apprenticeship nonetheless. The difference is the *thing into which* one is apprenticing.

Recall the delicate interior state that leisure consists of, resisting the pull of ratio so as to let the receptive intellectus faculty emerge. We can go through the motions of leisure, without realizing the internal goods of leisure. What we are apprenticing into is thus *not* the practice before us itself, but rather into leisure more generally. We do not need an expert to tell us how to wash the dishes. Rather, we need an expert or wise person to show us how to wash the dishes in a way that builds us up, activates our senses, enriches our experience, and enables leisure. We are apprenticing into a mode of experience, rather than a domain of action.

Most of us are not complete novices to leisure. Arguments on behalf of leisure work from within, as they speak to a restless self that is ever longing for rest. We often have an informed sense of what renewing leisure consists of (a walk, reading a book, even cleaning the house, a good night's rest), but we simply choose not to pursue it, or we pursue such activities in an unleisurely way. Most of us are weak-willed or what Greeks call *akratic* (Greek for "lacking command" or "weakness"). As akratics we may recognize what we should do vis-à-vis leisure, understanding what will renew our spirit, yet fall short. Our desires are often in conflict with what we know will renew us. The seductions of amusement culture and our weakness of will are formidable obstacles to the practice of leisure. They sabotage getting a practice of leisure off the ground and confound our ability to envision and hold in view what true leisure consists of. We are prone to losing our way, veering toward workaholism, on the one hand, or escapist amusement, on the other. Even more advanced practitioners of leisure need to be apprentices, submitting to systems and structures that support leisurely practice.

While often within reach, then, focal practices, as possible embodiments of leisure, require vision and communal accountability to see beyond what might appear dull, ordinary, and difficult. To the bored self, such practices indeed appear bland. Borgmann elaborates:

> Labor is exhausting, especially when it is divided. When we come home, we often feel drained and crippled. Diversion and pleasurable consumption appear to be consonant with this sort of disability. They promise to untie the knots and to soothe the aches. And so they do at a shallow level of our existence. At any rate, the call for exertion and engagement seems like a cruel and unjust demand. We have sat in the easy chair, beer at hand and television before us; when we felt stirrings of ambition, we found it easy to ignore our superego. (1987, p. 206)

This is option one – a familiar and well-trodden path. Yet more than an option, it becomes second-nature – a fixed ritual for attending to the weary self. Yet instead of this familiar ritual at the end of the day, Borgmann invites us to imagine option two – going for a walk outside on a cold day. For this to happen, we probably need someone to hold us accountable – someone who will not take no for an answer. Assuming our partner successfully prevails upon us to move in this direction, we might find ourselves annoyed, as we face the cold air. Borgmann elaborates:

> The discomfort was worse than we had thought. But gradually a transformation set in. Our gait became steady, our blood began to flow vigorously and wash away our tension,

we smelled the rain, began thoughtfully to speak with our companion, and finally returned home settled, alert, and with a fatigue that was capable of restful sleep. (1987, p. 26)

Focal practices, as possible embodiments of leisurely practice, are often within reach, but there is, especially for the novice, a high threshold to overcome. This is especially pertinent to the bored self, who is unable to see the possibilities latent within a focal practice. "The burdensome part of these activities," Borgmann notes, "is actually just the task of getting across a threshold of effort. As soon as you have crossed the threshold, the burden disappears" (2003, p. 23). Recall Kierkegaard's despair of necessity. The bored self is weighted down by necessity and is therefore without possibility. Simple tasks like walking, washing the dishes, or writing a letter appear dull and seem to offer little if anything to alleviate boredom, and yet once we begin to undertake them and settle in, renewing possibilities come into view. For this to happen though, Borgmann explains, a moral threshold or barrier must be surpassed:

Focal things and practices have a high threshold. The threshold is high morally not materially. It's not as if people have to exert themselves strenuously or face some danger before they can sit down at the table. It's right there, within reach. But there is a moral threshold. It's a bother, It's a pain. There is a high threshold, and so it's difficult to get across it. But once you're across it the reward is high as well. (2003, p. 25)

With amusement culture, by contrast, the thresholds (by design) are minimal, if any. I can easily and instantaneously enjoy the pleasure of watching a show or surfing the Internet. Yet, the rewards are far less than those that come with a focal practice. Borgmann has identified a key directive for the pursuit of leisure: Low threshold equals low reward; high threshold equals high reward.

The experience of leisure, as intrinsically valuable, is a high reward but requires effort and persistence. Given this, we need accountability – a friend, a partner, community – so as to develop the necessary practice and discipline that leisure requires. In this respect, we must surrender our freedom. The abdication of freedom that apprenticeship requires, however, is grounded in a deeper freedom to pursue a leisurely life. The rules or laws, so to speak, are not negative prohibitions but affirmative directives. They are guard rails to keep us on the right path. As an apprentice, we must counter the instinct to escape boredom by maximizing freedom – or what appears to be freedom. Freedom, in this respect, becomes a chain – chaining us to the despair of possibility. What is needed is commitment – a good chain that holds together possibility and necessity.[2]

This dynamic is incomprehensible to amateurs, who have as philosopher Ken Strike well notes, a limited ability "to cognize the worth of" leisurely practices, especially given our distracted state of mind (Strike, 2005). We must internalize the practice of leisure so as to ascertain its intrinsic goods. Simply presenting someone with a set of arguments on behalf of leisure will not work. What is needed, at this juncture, is trust (Strike, 2005). We need to trust the guidance of advanced practitioners of leisure and apprentice ourselves to their direction. We cannot think or argue our way into a new way of experiencing or living; rather, we must live our way into a new way of thinking. Novices are not able to see the point of leisure, because the capacity to see requires that certain habits of character (interior states of virtue) are already operative. Thus, the early stage of leisure development requires trust. This trust, however, is not entirely blind. It is driven or motivated by a firsthand experience with the misery of existential boredom. Born of this anguish, we long for something different and better, yet we know that we lack the imagination and the willpower to conceive of and choose a different course of action.

The second directive for cultivating leisure is maintaining a spirit of study. By study I am referring to its ancient conception, drawing especially on Aquinas' distinction between study (*studiositas*) and curiosity (*curiositas*). Curiosity, which is today largely regarded as a positive character disposition, was viewed in the ancient world as a budding vice. Augustine describes it as a

---

[2] Of course, talk of apprenticeship raises concerns about indoctrination. The key distinction to keep in mind is the end sought. Indoctrination seeks to fashion submissive selves. With apprenticeship, submission is a temporary stage toward maturity and developing responsible freedom. On this point, see especially Thiessen (1993), Warnick (2010), and Gary (2014).

disordered form of knowing. Yes, moved by curiosity we do seek to know in a certain way, but what we want to know, and why we want to know, Augustine sees as deeply problematic if not suspect. Curiosity, born of acedia, is "a disordered love of learning," or what Zena Hitz describes as a "love of spectacle" (Hitz, 2020, p. 250). Curious, we are prone to dabble in many things and easily drawn into the endless spin cycle. Hitz, drawing on Augustine, illuminates the direction and dynamics of the curious mind:

> *curiositas* includes the desire to know about the lives of people other than oneself; the desire for theatrics, to weep over imaginary sorrows; the desire to see a mangled corpse; the desire to look at circus freaks; the desire to see lizards catching flies, to see spiders entangling their prey, or to view barbaric gladiators shows. (Hitz, 2020, p. 250)

This summary, drawn from Augustine's confessions (circa. 397), powerfully resonates with the daily voyeurism of contemporary social media. Consuming and tracking contemporary news may often indulge a disordered appetite for knowledge. From this vantage point, Augustine would see this disordered state permeating most of what we consider to be just keeping informed.

Study (or studiositas), by contrast, was considered to be a virtuous form of knowing. Theologian Paul Griffiths (1955–present) describes it as a "disciplined appetite for knowledge" (2009, p. 13). As Aristotle notes in *Metaphysics*, to be human is to desire knowledge, yet this appetite, as its ready distortion into curiositas reveals, requires care and discipline. Our appetites, no matter how natural or potentially valuable, can easily become diffuse and disordered. Augustine's previous examples indicate where disordered appetites often lead us. The first step toward cultivating study is abstinence from intellectual voyeurism or rubbernecking – recognizing the pull such things have over us. Being studious requires continually checking our motivations. Reflecting on his own education, Augustine sees it shot through with curiositas – fueled by a desire to be clever more than wise, a desire to gawk at spectacle more than desire to inhabit a better way of life.

A key indicator of this is not simply the dubious value of the learning in question (e.g., gossip or learning to be clever), but an inability to stay focused on any one thing for very long – of what

Augustine describes as a lust for novelty. Study counters this flightiness. It is not, though, simply a negative abstaining from learning, but a positive disposition of the self for a deeper attention. Study in the monastic tradition, for example, involves removing many things so as to be able to focus on one thing deeply. To cultivate a spirit of study is to develop a capacity to attend to one thing (a task, a book, a walk) for a sustained period of time, being vigilant at resisting needless distractions.

The positive side of study is a committed, humble attentiveness. In order to do this, one must declutter and remove distractions that compromise attention. To be studious is to reign in unnecessary desires. It often requires physically decluttering our environment, with the aim of calming our restive minds, thus creating space for intellectus to enjoy the simplest of things. The monastic tradition is grounded in this insight: removing many things so as to fully attend to one thing.[3]

But rather than studious in this sense, the bored self is restless or prone to what the Buddhist tradition describes as "monkey-mind" – a tendency, both within and without, to flit from one thing to the next. Given this tendency, we are more curious than studious – easily drawn in by gossip and spectacle and all manner of trivial concerns. Rather than one focus of attention, the bored self is captivated by a multitude of interests. While this is not a new condition, the Internet has amplified and exacerbated this tendency. The monkey-mind within is now greeted by the monkey-mind without.[4]

Study usually connotes academic work: reading a book, solving an equation, or figuring out some problem. This connotation, though, is somewhat narrow. This kind of study should not be confined to a school or classroom. A spirit of studiositas should pervade every activity – reading, writing a letter, washing dishes, and pulling weeds. To undergo study, in this broader sense, is to be attentive and receptive – to be deeply engaged with and present to

[3] Monastic and priest Edmund Waldstein explains: "The monastic life is all about drawing back from that diversion—entering into a silence and monotony that allows us to really feel the pain of our spiritual loneliness. So that then we can let that pain be healed in the relation to God" (2020).
[4] This correlates with recent research on boredom (Hunter and Eastwood, 2018). Simply put, if we struggle with attention, we are more prone to suffer from boredom.

whatever it is one is undertaking. Nigella Lawson illuminates the salutary effects when a spirit of study is brought to the simple tasks required for preparing and cooking a meal:

> The routine busyness of all the peeling and chopping and stirring can be a balm for the buzzing brain. So many of the kitchen activities we might dread not because they are difficult but because they are monotonous – peeling two kilos of potatoes, say – are exactly what free us up, allowing us to relax or at least wind down a little. Of course, peeling a potato is not exactly mindless, but unless one has never peeled potatoes before, it is not something that requires hyper-vigilance. It's quietly absorbing. And as someone who is terminally fidgety, I am gratefully soothed by the many necessary low-level kitchen rituals that constitute cooking. Just enough focus is required to silence that chattering monkey-mind. Because one is doing something so familiar, so unthinkingly rehearsed, one isn't on high alert, but can let the senses – touch, smell, sight, sound – take over from intellect. (2020, p. 12)

Even such simple tasks as cleaning can be occasions to be studious – exercises that help focus the mind and help us let go of the preoccupations, worries, and distractions that often clutter the mind. The bored self, as Lawson notes, dreads the repetitive, monotonous tasks. Its monkey-mind wants constant stimulation and novelty, and yet it is precisely within these simple tasks, there is to be found "a balm for the buzzing brain." This repetitive simplicity creates space for an intellectus receptiveness that a more demanding, complex practice can mitigate against. This is why work can be so appealing. Recall Pascal's insight into boredom as fundamentally self-revulsion – both workaholism and escapist amusement temporarily unburden the self, but how they do so is the problem.

Two other conditions often qualify and enrich the spirit of study: silence and solitude. The act of leisure transpires within the recesses of a mind calmly engaged with a particular task. Leisurely beholding is easily disrupted by needless chatter and noise (both within and without). Study is nourished by silence and solitude. Yet often uncomfortable with both, we surround ourselves with noise and are easily drawn into chatter.[5] This is wisdom that we are losing fast, as we prioritize and make constant connection the norm. Yet such hyper-connectivity undermines study as the mind is ever poised to be interrupted, usually by something trivial. Given this propensity, the spirit of study can hardly begin to take root, as we unwittingly forgo the possibility of intellectus leisure. The quieting of the environment is needed to begin to quiet our monkey-mind.

In addition to apprenticeship and study, we need to develop tools for reflection that enable us to understand and name the experience of leisure. I describe this process as *contemplating or remembering epiphanies,* which aim to enlist both reason and vision. There is an especially precious and famous epiphany in Marcel Proust's *Remembrance of Things Past.* It consists of a revelation – of a forgotten memory – that is triggered when the narrator takes a bite out of madeleine – a rich cake usually served as a special treat on the weekends. Proust describes the event as follows,

> No sooner had the warm liquid mixed with the crumbs touched my palate than a shudder ran through me and I stopped, intent upon the extraordinary thing that was happening to me. An exquisite pleasure had invaded my senses, something isolated, detached, with no suggestion of its origin. And at once the vicissitudes of life had become indifferent to me, its disasters innocuous, its brevity illusory–this new sensation having had on me the effect which love has of filling me with a precious essence; or rather this essence was not in me it was me. Whence did it come? What did it mean? How could I seize and apprehend it? ... And suddenly the memory revealed itself. The taste was that of the little piece of madeleine which on Sunday mornings at Combray ... when I went to say good morning to her in her bedroom, my aunt Léonie used to give me. (1913–1927, p. 48)

Epiphanies are rare and precious moments of insight and revelation. In Proust's case, this epiphany is ushered in when he

---

[5] David Foster Wallace (2007) aptly describes the "Total Noise" that is the sound of the US culture – characterized by a "volume of info and spin and rhetoric" that exceeds our capacities "to make sense of or organize into any kind of triage of saliency or value."

recognizes, perhaps for the first time, what an exquisite gift his aunt used to prepare for him on Sunday mornings. It was love incarnate, literally, in the crumbs of a delicious treat. Epiphanies can range from a moment of aesthetic awareness to a eureka breakthrough in a field inquiry to an ethical realization. They are indeed precious and extraordinary moments of beholding – they are, leisure, in a nutshell.

The word epiphany comes from the Greek word, *epiphainein*, meaning "manifestation" or "revelation." While prominent within religious traditions, especially the Christian tradition, the concept of epiphany has moved well beyond its religious origins. Merriam-Webster (2021) offers two definitions. The first defines epiphany as a divine revelation. The second expands the notion to include, more broadly, any "illuminating discovery, realization, or disclosure." What is common to both definitions is the discontinuous nature of an epiphanic revelation. To experience an epiphany is to see something you were previously blind to. In this respect, also, there is something gifted about such experiences.

The Irish novelist and short-story writer James Joyce (1882–1941), in particular, is known for depicting epiphanic moments happening within the quotidian realties of day-to-day life – the simplest mundane object (such as Proust's madeleine) can occasion an epiphany. During such moments, Joyce explains, the soul of such objects, their whatness, leaps "to us from the vestment of its appearance" (Joyce, 1944, p. 58). Joyce elaborates: "The soul of the commonest object, the structure of which is so adjusted, seems to us radiant. The object achieves epiphany" (Joyce, 1944, p. 58). Epiphanies usher in the kind of seeing that is the apex of leisure – it is a flash of insight into the "miracle of life," which Hahn refers to. If leisure is fundamentally the act beholding; epiphanies are moments of supreme beholding. So precious are epiphanies that Joyce's protagonist Stephen Dedalus offers this telling counsel: "Remember your epiphanies on green oval leaves, deeply deep, copies to be sent if you died to all the great libraries of the world, including Alexandria" (Joyce, 1934/1990, p. 40).

In order to begin to realize a life of leisure, we must have a vision of leisure as a real possibility. An epiphany is an insight or revelation that captures our attention and summons us to become a better version of ourselves. We need to continually fund the imagination with specific stories and vignettes that illuminate the ideal we are striving for. We are prone to becoming careless – slipping often unawares into a state of acedia. To help remedy this tendency, we need to hold before our eyes moral examples or mirrors of edification.[6]

More than reasons, we are moved by that which is aesthetically compelling – a vision of a better self. Aspiring to be leisurely, we need to continually fund the imagination with compelling stories and vignettes that illuminate the ideal we are striving for. The notion of epiphany suggests a radical shift in orientation and perspective. While this is true, the need for epiphanic insight is continuous, given the default settings of obsessive work and escapist amusement. In this respect, we are like recovering addicts, often having to continually wean ourselves from a culture of total work and amusement. We need epiphanies again and again to continually see the possibilities for leisure. However, the recognition of epiphanies often requires assistance. We often need guides, helping us see what there is to see. As an embodied art form the life of leisure requires a certain disposition and sensibility to appreciate, to see, and to recognize its significance. We need docents who help us to recognize and name the experience of true leisure, noting the facets and subtle movements that incarnate leisurely practice.

Consider this vignette from the Vietnamese Buddhist monk and writer Thích Nhất Hạnh (1926–2022) on how to wash dishes in a leisurely way:

> While washing the dishes one should only be washing the dishes, which means that while washing the dishes one should be completely aware of the fact that one is washing the dishes. At first glance, that might seem a little silly: why put so much stress on a simple thing? But that's precisely the point. The fact that I am standing there and washing these bowls is a wondrous reality. I'm being completely myself, following my breath, conscious of my presence, and conscious of my thoughts and actions. There's no way I can be tossed around mindlessly like a bottle slapped here and there on the waves. (1987, pp. 3–4)

---

[6] More than simply looking up to or admiring a moral exemplar, an epiphany is a summons to become a certain kind of person (Gary and Chambers, 2021).

Hanh's imagery of a bottle tossed "around mindlessly" on the waves parallels the bored self, roving for something to engage with, "slapped here and there on the waves." By contrast, Hanh suggests that the leisurely self is attentive and engaged with "wondrous reality." Like so many tasks, this is a task we often simply want to be done with so we can move on to the next thing. Yet, Hanh redirects us to pursue this practice in a leisurely way:

> If while washing dishes, we think only of the cup of tea that awaits us, thus hurrying to get the dishes out of the way as if they were a nuisance, then we are not 'washing the dishes to wash the dishes'. What's more, we are not alive during the time we are washing the dishes. In fact, we are completely incapable of realizing the miracle of life while standing at the sink. If we can't wash the dishes, the chances are we won't be able to drink our tea either. (1987, pp. 3–4)

Hanh's vignette aims to provoke epiphanic awareness, yet it also provides a reasonable account of how a task as mundane as washing dishes is an opportunity for leisurely practice.

Such epiphanies need to be considered and reflected upon within a community of practitioners, calling us to engage such simple tasks in a leisurely way. The British novelist and philosopher Iris Murdoch (1919–1999) offers another poignant example:

> I am looking out of my window in an anxious and resentful state of mind, oblivious to my surroundings, brooding perhaps on some damage done to my prestige. Then suddenly I observe a hovering kestrel. In a moment everything is altered. The brooding self with its hurt vanity has disappeared. There is nothing now but kestrel. And when I return to thinking of the other matter it seems less important. And, of course, this is something which we may also do deliberately: give attention to nature in order to clear our minds of selfish care. (2014, p. 82)

Murdoch describes this process as "unselfing" – letting go of "the fat relentless ego" and its constant need for affirmation and status (2014, pp. 51 and 82). While Murdoch's moment with the kestrel might be prompted by a friend, directing her to look and see, her seeing requires that her mind be receptively engaged, undisturbed by chatter within or without. It requires silence and a moment of profound solitude. This is an exemplary account of moving from self-preoccupation into a state of leisure that enables beholding the word.

Murdoch's movement from self-brooding to seeing the glory of a kestrel illuminates a possible alternative way of embracing genuine leisure, but it sounds accidental. It is also just as likely that the kestrel could have gone unnoticed, with her anxieties and monkey-mind roiling within. How can such moments be orchestrated or their conditions primed? This is where a spirit of study brought to simple, mundane practices (reading a book or washing dishes) is especially helpful. The cure for monkey-mind in the monastic tradition does not involve injunctions to do more thinking, more reflecting, or more praying, but manual labor or simplistic repetitive prayers that require minimal ratio concentration.

Within the epiphanies cited, a spirit of grace is also pervasive – that is, the experience of leisure as a gift that we do not possess or control. Grace, from its religious context, means an unmerited gift. Recognizing and savoring what Hanh describes as "the miracle of life," is to embrace a spirit of grace. Even simple practices have intrinsic goods and can occasion an awareness of the "miracle of life." Leisurely attention is a form of lovely beholding. As an act of genuine presence and attention, it is an attempt to "to pierce the veil of selfish consciousness and join the world as it really is" (Murdoch, 2014, p. 91). "To love and admire anything outside yourself," novelist and essayist C. S. Lewis (1898–1963) explains, "is to take one step away from utter spiritual ruin" (2015, p. 127). What Lewis and Murdoch both underscore is that in striving toward leisure, we are not simply engaged with a particular act of leisure, but we are striving to become a certain kind of person – a humble person. Humility is often misunderstood as having a "modest or low view of oneself." Being genuinely humble is not to think of oneself at all, either critically or fawningly. It is an ability to see things objectively, letting go of the "fat relentless ego." It is a posture of openness, characterized by calm attentiveness.

So how might we educate for leisure? How do we cultivate leisure in our students? Implicitly, and explicitly, I have noted how digital media exacerbate the proclivities of the bored mind. Yet rather than offering a jeremiad against technology and social media, my aim throughout is to illuminate and contrast a bored way of being with a leisurely way of being, noting the deficits of the former, and the assets of the latter. While technology and digital media certainly enable and exacerbate the proclivities of the bored mind, epiphanic breakthroughs that reveal the flourishing possibilities of a leisurely way of being can and do come into view. Yet without discipline, and a supportive community, such moments will remain fleeting. The cultivation of leisure requires that we continually audit how technology impacts and forms our way of being, noting how it either supports or undermines our practice of genuine leisure.

6 CULTIVATING LEISURE

At this juncture, it is worth recalling the problem that animated this book. My central concern is the problem of boredom, and, in particular, the pervasive boredom experienced among students, especially in the middle- and high-school grades. Teachers share this concern: A classroom full of bored students can quickly become a management nightmare. We are conditioned to respond to boredom in one of two ways: avoidance or resignation. Both responses are learned behaviors that become ways of being, ways of inhabiting our world. We encounter a boring situation, and our first instinct is to escape it; failing this, we often turn toward resignation, surrendering possibilities for meaningful engagement.

When teachers seek to avoid boredom, they and their students are unwittingly conscripted into the boredom avoidance scheme. Teachers gravitate toward strategies that engage, amuse, stimulate, and entertain their students. They take this approach for the simple reason that it is "effective" – it helps temporarily mitigate students' boredom. Kierkegaard diagnoses this strategy as the despair of possibility. This variant of despair is marked by an escapism that is perpetually unsatisfied with what is.

When teachers employ the second strategy, resignation, they convey implicitly (and sometimes explicitly) to their students that life will be boring, and they must accept this brute fact. With sheer authority, cajoling, threats, and routine inertia, teachers make their students comply. Mundane, seemingly pointless tasks, while bleak, help pass the time, providing a low-level form of engagement. Something is better than nothing. This mindset is the despair of necessity that Kierkegaard diagnoses. Such despair is marked by a gradual lowering of expectations. Both strategies, escapism and resignation, incapacitate us for leisure. When we choose boredom avoidance, we lack the patience to attend to what is in front of us. When we give in to resignation, we put up with or push through tasks that need to be done, but lose sight of the possibilities for meaningful engagement.

Leisure and Education

Contending with boredom, we are conditioned to imagine just a few basic movements: busywork, escapist amusement, or a Sisyphean resignation to the work–amusement treadmill. Recall how boredom impoverishes the imagination and the will. We have trouble envisioning a viable alternative way of being (the despair of necessity), and, to the extent that we do envision that alternative way, we lack the drive to execute it (the despair of possibility). But there is a third way. Rather than thinking of boredom as something to be avoided or endured, we can think of boredom as a harbinger of meaning. Boredom has something to teach us. Thinking of this third way can help teachers initiate students into a leisurely way of being.

The 1918 Cardinal Principles on Secondary Education, discussed in Chapter 1, included leisure as an essential aim for education. The document's drafters recognized that countless individuals, especially in urban centers, lacked the resources and imagination to pursue leisure. This situation created systemic social problems, especially alcoholism (recall that the Cardinal report was issued just two years prior to Prohibition). A century later, whether intentionally or not, schools have abandoned leisure as a worthwhile objective. And yet, the existential imperative for leisure education is more pressing than ever. The contemporary problems associated with chronic boredom avoidance have been studied and are well documented (Biolcati et al., 2018; Crockett et al., 2015; Lee and Zelman, 2019; LePera, 2011; Mercer and Eastwood, 2010). The larger consumer culture, rather than solving this problem, only exacerbates it. The leisure tradition, conversely, provides a way to address existential problems that undermine personal and communal flourishing. Boredom avoidance, even in its more "innocuous" forms, is associated with a nagging restlessness that encourages excessive consumption, which our planet cannot sustain. We are conditioned to consume and spend our way out of this problem. Pope Francis offers this counter vision of a person capable of leisure:

> In reality, those who enjoy more and live better each moment are those who have given up dipping here and there, always on the lookout for what they do not have. They experience what it means to appreciate each person and each thing, learning familiarity with the simplest things and how to enjoy them. So they are able to shed unsatisfied needs, reducing their obsessiveness and weariness. Even living on little, they can live a lot, above all when they cultivate other pleasures and find satisfaction in fraternal encounters, in service, in developing their gifts, in music and art, in contact with nature, in prayer. Happiness means knowing how to limit some needs which only diminish us, and being open to the many different possibilities which life can offer. (2015)

In this vision, two key movements or habits stand out: simplicity of heart and gratitude. Simplicity of heart refers to an ability to refrain from needless things, keeping fickle desires in check. This is what a spirit of study entails. Such simplicity enables space for intellectus reception. The second movement is gratitude – an active capacity to recognize, appreciate, and enjoy people and familiar things. Leisure provides access to forms of pleasure that are more sustainable as we "learn familiarity with the simplest things and how to enjoy them" (Francis, 2015).

The turn, though, to leisure is difficult. It involves the constant project of properly ordering and reordering our affections and desires. This requires curbing certain desires so as to give birth to new ones. To begin this process, we need to apprentice ourselves to role models and exemplars we trust, cultivate a spirit of study, and contemplate narratives of epiphany for renewed inspiration and direction. Arguments on behalf of leisure are understandably greeted with skepticism. Given the utilitarian logic that prevails within schools – with its hyper-focus on standardization and testing – the cultivation of leisure sounds improbable at best. Schools and teachers are pressed to deliver on ratio outcomes at the expense of intellectus learning.

Restoring a focus on leisure in modern schools, philosopher of education and public-school teacher Sean Steel correctly argues, requires a transformation in how we think about education (2014). The Common Core vision, as noted in Chapter 1, focuses exclusively on ratio or discursive learning, with hardly a nod to intellectus (or contemplative) forms of knowing. Yet this hyper-pragmatism conflicts with another reality: Even before the COVID pandemic, students were experiencing alarming rates of anxiety, aimlessness, addiction, depression, and suicidal ideation – as were teachers (Flannery, 2018). Moreover, teachers are caught in the middle, pressed to deliver on ratio outcomes (which prioritize criticizing and analyzing versus contemplating and appreciating), while facing students who suffer various degrees of despair. Leisure is not a panacea for all the ills that plague us, but it is a vital constituent of human flourishing, and it takes direct aim at the neuroses that pervade modern life.

In the rest of this chapter, I consider the outlines of a pedagogy for leisure, offering examples that aim to show, more than tell, what a leisure-informed pedagogy looks like. While there is no surefire recipe or formula for leisure, certain parameters can help us cultivate leisure. The three guidelines outlined in Chapter 5 – apprenticeship, study, and epiphany – are present in all three examples noted below, but each illustrates one particular guideline more prominently than the others.

The Trusting Apprentice

Education as a form of apprenticeship is an ancient idea. We see the paradigm of the wise elder apprenticing or initiating novices into practices across various traditions and contexts. It is particularly prominent in religious contexts, but it is also a key feature within craft traditions. While industrialization has largely disrupted the apprenticeship model, it continues to thrive in some spaces. Certain trades, given their complexity and the enduring need for practical wisdom, cannot be fully automated.[1] The expert master, informed by practical wisdom, remains essential.

---

[1] Again, on this point, see especially Matthew Crawford's *Shop Class as Soulcraft: An Inquiry into the Value of Work* (2010).

As noted in Chapter 5, novices need apprenticeship because they have only a partial understanding of the goods internal to a practice. Given this, they need to trust expert direction. As Strike notes, "Students cannot judge the worth of intellectual practices until they have moved some distance down the path of initiation into them" (2005, p. 232). Strike focuses on intellectual practices, but the same is true of simpler practices, including types of manual labor, and even walking and washing dishes, if – that is – they are to yield the insights that Borgmann and Hahn report in carrying out these tasks.

Given the limited perception of apprentices (namely, practical insight into intrinsic goods), they need to be able to trust those who are instructing them. Trust is the "epistemic bridge" required to advance (Strike, 2005, p. 232). In order to understand, we must first trust the insight of a superior guiding us into performing a practice in the right way. The movie *The Karate Kid* offers an iconic illustration of education as initiation, underscoring the importance of being a faithful or trusting apprentice (Avildsen, 1984). The main character, Daniel LaRusso, is being bullied at school by a group of arrogant thugs. He discovers that his neighbor, Mr. Miyagi, in addition to being a handyman for the apartment complex where Daniel and his mother live, is also a martial arts expert. Daniel implores Mr. Miyagi to teach him karate so he can defend himself. Mr. Miyagi agrees – but only after setting the terms of their mentor–apprentice relationship. This exchange is worth quoting in full:

> MIYAGI: First make sacred pact; I promise teach karate. That's my part. You promise learn. I say, you do – no questions. That's your part. Deal?
>
> DANIEL: It's a deal.
>
> MIYAGI: First wash all the cars, then wax (Avildsen, 1984).

Immediately when Mr. Miyagi's instruction begins, Daniel begins to question it. "Why do I have to?" he asks. Mr. Miyagi promptly reminds him: "Remember deal. No questions." Mr. Miyagi then demonstrates the proper technique for waxing cars, which, to Daniel, appears ludicrous. Mr. Miyagi carefully instructs Daniel to wax on with the right hand and wax off with the left hand, breathing in through his nose while waxing. "Don't forget to breathe," Mr. Miyagi says, "Very important."

Somewhat grudgingly Daniel settles into the work. On occasion, Mr. Miyagi corrects him, reminding Daniel of the proper technique. Daniel's unenthusiastic attitude is evidence that – although he trusts Miyagi enough to continue to follow his instructions – he is still not fully convinced that what he is being told to do is helping him reach his goal. This is a familiar response of apprentices toward practices, and it has an important connection to boredom. In this stage, the apprentice will be susceptible to a variety of negative psychological experiences, one of which is boredom with the seemingly monotonous and unimportant tasks of learning. And yet, boredom experienced *within* an apprenticeship differs from the boredom experienced outside of one. The teacher is there for support and encouragement if the student falls into a bout of boredom, and if the instructor is not there, then the goal-oriented structure of the apprenticeship promises to provide support for the apprentice's continued engagement.

The instruction continues, with Mr. Miyagi directing Daniel to sand floors and paint fences, again providing specific instructions on how to do each specific task. Daniel complies, but after a few days he becomes impatient, and his trust reaches a breaking point. "Four days I've been busting my ass," he grumbles. "I haven't learned a thing." Mr. Miyagi responds: "You learn plenty." Daniel continues to complain, saying all he has learned is how to sand Mr. Miyagi's deck, wash his cars, and paint his fence. Mr. Miyagi responds, saying, "Not everything is as seems."

Frustrated, Daniel decides to break the deal and go home. At this point, Mr. Miyagi intervenes directly, calling Daniel, insisting that he show him the "sand the floor" movement, followed by the "wax on" and "wax off" movements, and then the "paint the fence" movement. Daniel halfheartedly and sarcastically goes through the motions. Mr. Miyagi gently scolds him, correcting his technique. This scene builds to an epiphany as Mr. Miyagi then calls for the gesture "wax on" and throws a punch at Daniel, which Daniel easily blocks. Mr. Miyagi then picks up the pace, throwing punches and kicks, all of which Daniel is easily able to fend off with "wax on," "sand the floor," and "paint the fence" movements.

The wisdom of Mr. Miyagi's statement, "Not everything is as seems," becomes evident as Daniel recognizes that each movement is a fundamental building block in his martial arts training. Mr. Miyagi's fastidious insistence on proper form becomes, in that moment, clear to Daniel. While this is a made-for-Hollywood epiphany, it illuminates the process of initiation. Mr. Miyagi is not able to directly explain his methodology in a form that Daniel can comprehend at the outset. Even if Daniel were to say he understood at the start, his affirmation, at this early stage, would convey trust rather than actual understanding. Crawford illumines the dynamics in play:

> For the apprentice there is a progressive revelation for the reasonableness of the master's actions. He may not know why things have to be done a certain way at first, and have to take it on faith, but the rationale becomes apparent as he gains experience. (2010, p. 159)

Daniel, through doing, comes to recognize the point of the exercises he has been undertaking. This realization was contingent upon his acquiring a certain proficiency with each move, so he could experience firsthand the actual power in play. In order for this to happen, he needed to follow Miyagi's directions on faith. Again, trust is the "epistemological bridge." The apprentice must trust the expert in order to make progress. Yet such trust, rather than a surrender of autonomy, is "the basis on which his submission to the judgments of a master feel ennobling rather than debasing" (Crawford, 2010, p. 160). It is a bridge toward a masterful autonomy.

The trope of the impatient novice confronting the wise master is familiar in education. Education as initiation is more clearly on display in the trades, but it exists in most learning contexts, whether the subject is carpentry, math, or chemistry. Students new to a discipline must encounter and become familiar with a sub-world rich with new terms. To the neophyte, the advanced structure of a discipline initially does not make sense and must be largely taken on faith. Such trust is required even in fields that are presumably founded on "empirical" truth. Learning chemistry, for example, requires accepting, at face value, a peculiar nomenclature (moles, the periodic table) and imaging properties of elements operating at an atomic level.

The importance of building trust arises early in education. It begins to emerge when students ask the simple yet direct question,

"Why do I have to learn this?" or, phrased slightly differently, "What's the point of this?" Teachers and administrators can evade the spirit of this question by pointing to school requirements as an answer – because it is in the textbook or required by state standards. We can also evade the spirit of the question by appealing to external goods, answering that the point of learning something is to earn a high grade, get into a prestigious college, or land a well-paying job. Each of these responses largely suggests that students should learn this material because it will help them acquire external goods. Teachers are effectively asking students to trust that this particular task or assignment is valuable preparation for success in the world. Failing this, there is an appeal to self-interest with a view toward the status and future success that correlates with academic achievement.

The trust required of an apprentice, by contrast, is qualitatively different. Rather than trusting that what they're being asked to learn will lead to extrinsic goods, the apprentice must trust that what they are being asked to learn will lead to intrinsic goods. The apprentice needs to trust that they are learning new ways of seeing and acting that they will come to appreciate over time. Essentially, the expert is saying, "Trust and commit to the process, and you will become a different person who sees in a different way." While many students have already experienced a variety of extrinsic goods and directly understand their appeal, the intrinsic goods of a new practice are often beyond their view and understanding. The trust required of an apprentice is the first step, not with a view toward some future distant good, but amounts to a call to attend carefully to what is before them. In the case of Daniel, he was called to trust the process of carefully sanding floors and waxing cars. Looking ahead to his goal of becoming a karate master might actually impede careful attention to the necessary tasks before him. He must first appreciate the intrinsic goods of these simple moves. Thus, the appeal to extrinsic or intrinsic goods can call forth different kinds or degrees of attention. By leveraging an extrinsic good or reward, teachers may unwittingly divide students' attention, compromising the focus needed to appreciate the intrinsic goods of the practices before them. As noted, the progressive educator seeks to steer clear of this issue altogether, designing learning experiences that are so intrinsically engaging and meaningful that questions about purpose and relevance do not arise. Yet, this approach inevitably comes up short. Most practices, if not all, require repetition of simple and tedious drills.

The trust required for leisure is still more complex. A novice studying carpentry clearly recognizes the gaps in her knowledge. Given this, she accepts that she will need to learn from an expert. An expert's authority is on display in their handiwork and finished products (e.g., a well-crafted desk). Over a period of time, the apprentice too can become a master carpenter and then possess the knowledge and practical wisdom of an expert. Once a person achieves expertise as a violinist, a chemist, or a surgeon, that skill set, assuming the person remains in good health and of sound mind, remains largely intact. It might atrophy over time with a lack of practice, but the foundation endures.

With leisure, the skills and practical wisdom developed are more elusive. We do not possess them in the same way. It is a form of what Kierkegaard describes as subjective versus objective truth. A master carpenter can objectively say, "I am an excellent carpenter." There are clear standards to assess the accuracy of this statement. This same kind of confident self-assessment is out of place for the practitioner of leisure. Recall that leisure is a state of gratitude and intellectus receptivity. It is not a skill or knowledge base that we acquire and possess. Rather, it is a learned posture that is fragile and difficult to sustain. An advanced disciple of leisure recognizes that in the truest sense, we are all apprentices to leisure.

At the same time, teachers can do several things to help students apprentice into the fragile tasks of leisure. Although there are no leisure "experts," some people have developed rituals in their lives that make space for intellectus receptivity. These individuals will admit – and this is the important point – that there is never a guarantee one will receive the insight, the peace of mind, the reorientation of things that one may hope for in performing these rituals. We are, in this sense, always "on the way." There are moments of arrival – of intellectus peace – but these are passing. As Kierkegaard notes, becoming a self is a constant work in progress. But we can improve our sensitivity to the world around us such that we are much more responsive to the sources of meaning and value that the leisurely mind can appreciate. How this can be done, I hope, will become clear in the following two sections.

Cultivating a Spirit of Study

Study, as noted in Chapter 5, is defined in opposition to being curiosity. Curiositas is marked by restlessness and superficiality. It is a desire to be in the know – to be caught up with the daily stream of news and gossip. Roving curiosity is a symptom of existential boredom. Curiosity seems innocuous, yet even its mild forms undermine the deep attention that leisure requires. When we give in to curiosity, we give in to irrelevant forms of knowing. To be curious is to be on the hunt for novelty, whether it is a breaking news story, a sports score, a text, or an email. There is so much for the curious mind to tend to.

Studiositas, as noted, is redeemed or transformed curiositas. To be studious is to limit clutter, distraction, and trivial pursuits. This negation or restraint, though, is animated by a positive desire to attend to something carefully. To be studious is to cultivate deep attention. It requires auditing one's context to ensure optimal listening. Becoming studious requires unlearning the habits of curiosity.

Recall that the first movement in leisurely practice is attention, carefully directed and sustained. The leisurely mind is the opposite of the curious, monkey-mind that flits from one thing to the next. Calling forth attention is the recursive movement that occurs in classrooms every day; a teacher summons students to attend to something: an assignment, a demonstration, verbal or written instructions, and so on. At its most elementary level, the process of education is guiding students to learn how to pay attention. We take this movement for granted, and yet it is the foundation of learning. Before we can process, interpret, analyze, or critique, we must simply learn how to pay attention. Without it, nothing of substance can follow.

The best teachers are masters at directing and holding students' attention. To enter a master teacher's classroom is to witness a liturgy (the use of images, rituals, and symbols in addition to explicit directives) that carefully cultivates, directs, and develops students' attention. Every aspect of the teacher's words and gestures – where she stands, the design of the room, and the arrangement of the desks – direct and hold students' attention. Students, accordingly, become acclimated to the rhythms and directives of the class: They know where to focus and when to do so.

The kind of attention that modern schools prioritize is largely ratio-focused. Students are taught to assess, analyze, evaluate, interpret, integrate, demonstrate, apply, compare, critique, and so on – all ratio forms of knowing. To cultivate a spirit of study is to ensure both ratio and intellectus forms of knowing are nurtured. Toward this end, teachers should help students clearly and mindfully cultivate appreciation, wonder, and admiration. Consider, for example, one class project that Joanna Ziegler (1950–2010) assigned to her college students. Ziegler, an art historian, taught at the College of the Holy Cross before her untimely death due to pancreatic cancer in 2010.

Ziegler recognized how prone to distraction her students were. She also recognized the limits of ratio-fixated learning. Specifically, she noted how this kind of learning impaired the quality of attention students were able to give to artistic creations. Aiming to help them deepen their attention skills, Ziegler set up a semester-long class that exclusively cultivated intellectus. Students in her class were required to visit a local museum in Worcester, Massachusetts. Once there, they were given a choice of one of three paintings by: "Thomas Gainsborough (English, eighteenth century portraitist and landscape painter), Claude Monet (the French Impressionist), or Robert Motherwell (American Abstract Expressionist)" (2001, p. 38). Each week, for thirteen weeks, the students had to visit their painting in person, sit in the same place, at the same time, and view it for at least an hour. And each week, they had to submit a five-page paper about what they saw. "Thirteen weeks, thirteen papers in all – each essentially the same, but reworked, refined, and rewritten" (2001, p. 38). The students were not to consult any outside sources, but rather to see for themselves.

As expected, the students resisted the assignment. Many were irked by the repetitive nature of the work. While they understood the need for repetition to become proficient at a sport or an instrument, they failed to see the point of this assignment. Yet as the weeks went on, Ziegler noticed a transformation in students' essays. The accounts, she notes, moved from:

> personalized, almost narcissistic, responses to descriptions firmly grounded in the picture. Descriptions evolved from being fraught with willful interpretation, indeed selfishness

(students actually expressed hostility at being made to go to the Museum once a week), to revealing some truth about the painting on its own terms. Most importantly, students developed a personal relationship with what became known as "my" work of art. It was a work they knew by heart, could describe from memory—brushstroke, color change, and subtlety of surface texture. Through repeated, habitual, and direct experience (not working from slides or photographs but confronting the real work of art), students were transformed from superficial spectators ... into skilled, disciplined beholders with a genuine claim to a deep and intimate knowledge of a single work of art—and they knew it. (2001, p. 37)

Ziegler makes several noteworthy moves with this assignment. Four stand out: limiting choice, ensuring physical presence, cultivating ritual observance, and maintaining solitude. First, the fact that Ziegler limited the range of attending objects was significant. One can imagine having students write about a different painting each week across several genres. While there is merit in this approach, it is fundamentally different from the approach she takes. Recall that the bored mind seeks to maximize autonomy by keeping options open. While perhaps not thinking about it in terms of situational and existential boredom, Ziegler, by limiting her students' choices, takes direct aim at the proclivities of the bored mind. This assignment binds the students to one thing.

Given the numerous standards students are expected to master and the pressure teachers feel to introduce content, Ziegler's assignment is daring, to say the least. And yet, it is also simple in its conception and execution: sit with and write about something worth seeing and be sure *to see it.* Awakening and prompting students to utilize their capacity for sustained attention was Ziegler's overarching goal. Her lesson was also studious in requiring *physical presence.* Physically sitting or standing in front of a painting is an entirely different experience than viewing it on a smartphone or laptop. This simple ritual of physically going to the museum effectively structured and guided attention. Art museums are places of quiet. Also, physical presence enables the students, as beholders, to see the texture and grain of the paint.

In addition, Ziegler's demand for repetition was critical. Her overarching aim with this assignment was for the students to become "practiced beholders." For this to begin to take hold, a routine and a ritual – a practice – needed to be established, so students would "enter into a work of art as a thing in its own right." Historian Jonathan Z. Smith captures what is at stake in simple rituals like this. Ritual, Smith notes, "is, first and foremost, a mode of paying attention. It is a process of marking interest ... It is this characteristic, as well, that explains the role of place as a fundamental component of ritual: place directs attention" (1992, p. 103). This is effectively what Ziegler is up to.

Also significant is Ziegler's requirement for solitude. Students were required to spend time *alone* with their painting, to see it for themselves and by themselves. This runs counter to trends in education, which increasingly emphasize collaborative approaches to learning. While often pedagogically appropriate, collaborative learning or group work mitigates against intellectus attending, which is fragile and easily disrupted by chatter, self-consciousness, and posturing for peers. Moments of leisure with a book, with a painting, in nature, or washing dishes entail solitude.

While the students in Ziegler's class perhaps did not conceive of themselves as apprentices, an apprenticeship was, in fact, what Ziegler had set up. She was guiding students into a practice that at first seemed strange and peculiar to them. At the outset, few of the students, if any, could perceive the value in this endeavor. Beginning to appreciate the intrinsic goods requires being a faithful apprentice, trusting the practical wisdom of the teacher. Ultimately, these structures and rituals served to transform how and what the students saw. Recall that leisure in its most compelling sense is a form of experience in which we are (1) attentive, as we encounter a saturated phenomenon; (2) receptive, as we engage our intellectus faculty, while resisting the pull of our busy ratio faculty; and (3) ultimately, transformative as ratio gives way to intellectus beholding. Ziegler apprenticed students into these three movements.

To be sure, these steps are not automatic. They require a receptive willingness. To the extent that Ziegler's students were willing to take these steps, the object they were considering (the painting) was no longer merely an image to be looked at, but rather was what philosopher Jean-Luc Marion describes as an icon

(2002). The more that we gaze at or address an icon, the more the icon addresses us. To behold icons, notes Marion, is to recognize saturated phenomena, which surpass our controlling ego. Our horizons are overwhelmed. We become "more the subject constituted by its givenness than it is the object constituted" by our subjectivity (Westphal, 2003, p. 26). To such phenomena, we return again and again for insight, for purpose, for enlightenment, and for transformation. Ziegler's pedagogy aims to cultivate a spirit of study. This is evident in the simplicity of the task she has the students undertaken. The limitations she puts in place – especially limiting distractions – scaffold a deeper kind of beholding. More than criticizing, comparing, contrasting, or evaluating, Ziegler sought to cultivate in her students wonder, deep attention, and ultimately a capacity for leisure.

Remember Your Epiphanies

Contemplating or remembering epiphanies is the third directive for cultivating leisure. The first two directives are aimed at the students – recognizing the value of the apprenticeship model and the importance of cultivating a spirit of study to nurture intellectus receptivity. This third directive is intended for teachers. While great teachers aim to prime and provoke epiphanies in their students – cultivating eureka moments of insight, wonder, and intrigue – my interest with respect to leisure is calling forth the importance of remembering our own epiphanies. The bored mind has become immune to epiphanic breakthrough – there is nothing new to see. It has, simply put, forgotten its epiphanies. It needs to retrieve them – to recollect the "deeply deep" epiphanies, as Joyce describes them, that have receded from view (1934/1990, p. 40). If the present environment seems to offer little in the way of stimulation and meaningful engagement, remembering such epiphanies can break boredom's stifling spell. An epiphany, to quote Franz Kafka, is an "axe for the frozen sea within us" (1904/1977, p. 52). It disrupts a way of seeing that is ever on the lookout for novelty and is blind to possibilities in front of us.

An epiphanic way of seeing pushes against the normal run of things, where we seek to quickly size things up and move on. To counter this tendency, the teacher, first and foremost, must herself be engaged with the animating questions of her discipline. If a teacher can ever hope to occasion wonder or deep appreciation for her field of inquiry, she must embody this herself. Her animating passion needs to be tended to and protected. The demands of the teaching endeavor, the institutional drag, and the daily confrontation with indifferent students can chip away at the pathos that first inspired a teacher's love for her discipline. Writer Andre Dubus (1936–1999), in his short story "Dancing After Hours," captures the familiar burnout in his portrait of Emily, an English teacher, who gives up teaching:

> [Emily] had stopped teaching because of pain: she had gone with passion to high school students, year after year, and always there was one student, or even five, who wanted to feel a poem or story or novel, and see more clearly because of it. But Emily's passion dissolved in the other students. They were young and robust, and although she knew their apathy was above all a sign of their being confined by classrooms and adolescence, it still felt like apathy. It made Emily feel isolated and futile…. In her last three years of teaching she realized she was becoming scornful and bitter, and she worked to control the tone of her voice, and what she said to students, and what she wrote on their papers. She taught without confidence or hope, and felt like a woman standing at a roadside, reading poems aloud into the wind as cars filled with teenagers went speeding by…. She did not want to teach again, or work with teenagers, or have to talk to anyone, about the books she read. But she knew that pain had defeated her, while other teachers had endured it, or not felt it as sharply. (1996, pp. 210–211)

Teacher burnout is a common problem, more so today than ever. More problematic than teacher burnout is what philosopher of education Chris Higgins describes as teacher "burn-in" (2011, p. 153). These are teachers who, unlike Emily, stay in the work rather than leave, perhaps because they feel trapped or simply need the paycheck. Such teachers risk becoming cynical – indifferent to whether students are engaged or not, treating the work as a checklist they must get through each day. They become proficient at going through the motions, but have given up any greater aspiration to move students to appreciate, in a substantive way, what they are teaching. Burning out, or burning in, is not unique to the teaching profession. It is a variant of existential boredom – a weariness with life. That which has inspired no longer does so. For the teaching endeavor, however, this experience is especially tragic. More than teaching content, an indifferent teacher teaches indifference. Rather than appreciating fields of study as saturated phenomena that are situated in and sustained by focal practices, indifferent teachers perceive these subjects as, at best, necessarily useful for some future work.

An epiphany requires a certain degree of openness to seeing something and to being moved. Treating or regarding subjects as mere preparation for future work, or simply as pointless busywork, closes off the possibility of an epiphanic breakthrough. Thus, the cultivation of epiphanies must begin with the teacher – with her reawakening and reliving her own epiphanies. Teachers who leave because of burnout or who stay and become cynical because of burn-in are understandably responding to the demands of the work and the desire to protect oneself. While the indifference of Emily's students is not personal, Emily cannot help but experience it as personal. To cultivate epiphanies, one must remember their own epiphanies – to continually return to the source of that inspiration, resisting the forces of indifference, on the one hand, or crass pragmatism, on the other.

Plato's metaphor of the cave can offer us insight here. Recall the moment when the freed prisoner, taking in the sun and splendor of nature, recollects his former situation. He sees the cave facade for what it was, and sees through the petty games he was immersed in, competing with his peers at identifying shadows on the wall. Yet, he is also moved with compassion as he thinks about his former fellow cave dwellers. The motive to teach is animated by a desire to share the epiphanies that we have witnessed with others. Yet, this cannot be forced. In fact, in Plato's account, the freed prisoner's attempts to liberate his colleagues are met with resistance, even scorn and persecution. So teachers too often face students' indifference and even hostility to what they are offering. Plato's cave, though it is a cave, is a comfort zone for the cave dwellers. To maintain her resolve, the teacher must remember the light outside of the cave – the epiphanies she has experienced. If she neglects this, despair is likely to take hold in the form of lost meaning and purpose. More significantly, this teacher loses the opportunity to cultivate epiphanies for her students.

The metaphor of a teacher as a kind of mediator comes into view – one who mediates the surpassing beauty and complexity of her discipline, remembering and revisiting the epiphanies that inspired her along the way. Rather than seeming old and faded, such epiphanies renew. Appreciating the beauty of a poem or the brilliance of Newton's laws of motion can recur again and again. What is at stake is seeing one's discipline as a saturated phenomenon, ultimately witnessing how one properly encounters a saturated phenomenon – with reverence, awe, and wonder. Of course, the teacher must turn to her particular students, considering their age, temperament, prior knowledge, and more, so as to discern how best to convey content, but the first and most critical move is for the teacher to be a constant beholder of beauty: to recollect and contemplate the epiphanies that brought her out of the cave. The teacher cannot give what she does not have. If the subject in question has become dull, stagnant, lifeless, or is simply turned into a list of learning outcomes to be checked off, occasioning an epiphany is unlikely.

EPILOGUE
Coda on the Self at Leisure

Nietzsche's idea of eternal recurrence brings the question of boredom into clear view. Intended as a hypothetical thought experiment, Nietzsche (1844–1900) asks us to imagine:

> If some day or night a demon were to steal after you into your loneliest loneliness and say to you: "This life as you now live it and have lived it, you will have to live once more and innumerable times more; and there will be nothing new in it, but every pain and every joy and every thought and sigh and everything unutterably small or great in your life will have to return to you, all in the same succession and sequence" ... Would you not throw yourself down and gnash your teeth and curse the demon who spoke thus? Or have you once experienced a tremendous moment when you would have answered him: "You are a god and never have I heard anything more divine." (1882/1974, p. 273)

This is the recipe for eternal boredom – being tethered to doing the same thing over and over again. Yet more than the pain of under-stimulation, Nietzsche suggests that the real discomfort and dread of boredom involves being stuck with oneself. This parallels Kierkegaard's formula for despair: "To will to be rid of oneself" (1980, p. 72). When we avoid boredom, we are seeking to avoid ourselves.

Yet what if, instead of despising ourself, we love ourself? In this case, Nietzsche suggests, eternal recurrence would be a blessing. This conjecture is intended to provoke reflection and

action, daring us to live the kind of life that we would be content
to choose to live for an eternity. The question, which Nietzsche
says we should feel as a great weight upon every decision, is:
"Do you desire this once more and innumerable times more?"
(1882/1974, p. 274). This might sound like a call to live out a
bucket list – to fashion a life full of travel, interesting pursuits,
and so forth. And yet, would this not be a version of Kierkegaard's aesthetic sphere – a life ultimately driven by boredom
avoidance and marked by despair? Imagining despair-free existence, Kierkegaard offers this elliptical vision:

> The formula that describes the state of the self when despair
> is completely rooted out is this: in relating itself to itself and
> in willing to be oneself, the self rests transparently in the
> power that established it. (1983, p. 14)

This way of being includes both an active and passive movement.
The self must actively synthesize necessity and possibility, steering
clear of the despair that afflicts both extremes. And yet the self must
also be capable of resting – of resting "in the power that established
it" – which is to say resting in God. Towards this end, the self must
be able to love itself – to appreciate the sheer marvel the self is. This
is not self-centered egotism, but an intellectus turning toward the
world and the self – a beholding, accepting, and loving the self and
world as they are.

The bored self struggles with both movements. It is characterized by a constant restlessness that is driven by self-loathing
in both its mild and extreme forms. The protagonist in *Diary of a
Country Priest* by French novelist George Bernanos (1888–1948)
illuminates this dynamic:

> So I said to myself that people are consumed by boredom.
> Naturally, one has to ponder for a while to realise this—
> one does not see it immediately. It is like some sort of dust.
> One comes and goes without seeing it, one breathes it in,
> one eats it, one drinks it, and it is so fine that it doesn't
> even scrunch between one's teeth. But if one stops up for
> a moment, it settles like a blanket over the face and hands.
> One has to constantly shake this ash-rain off one. That is
> why people are so restless. (1974, p. 7)

Echoing Kierkegaard, Bernanos traces the root of boredom to rest-lessness and the root of restlessness to despair or self-loathing. The bored, restless self is unable to rest. And yet, by the end of the story, Bernanos's country priest finds a way out of this negative loop:

> The strange mistrust I had of myself, of my own being, has flown, I believe forever. That conflict is done. I cannot understand it anymore. I am reconciled to myself. To the poor shell of me. How easy it is to hate oneself! True grace is to forget. Yet if pride could die in us the supreme grace would be to love oneself in all simplicity. (1974, p. 314)

How easy it is, Bernanos notes, to hate oneself. The ability to love oneself, without egotism, is a key part of the transition from a bored state to a leisurely state. Where self-hate appears to be the under-lying ground of the bored state; love appears to be the bedrock of the leisure state.

The film *Groundhog Day* illustrates this contrast and transition in an amusing and perceptive way. Its protagonist, Phil Connors, moves from a despairing, self-loathing, bored state to a despair-free, loving, self-loving, leisured state. Phil finds him-self trapped in the town of Punxsutawney, Pennsylvania, having to repeat the same day – February 2 – again and again. Each day he wakes up, and it is once again Punxsutawney's annual Ground-hog Day celebration. At first, he is understandably alarmed and distressed by the situation, but then he begins to revel in his fore-knowledge of the day's events. He exploits what he knows to live out his wildest fantasies without consequence, knowing that he will only wake up to the same day. Eventually, though, this strategy to pass and enjoy the time – which is Kierkegaard's aesthete in action – runs its course. The transgressions and trysts that he manufactures eventually lose their novelty.

What first was maddening and then appeared to be filled with endless, exciting possibilities eventually becomes Sylvia Plath's "infinitely desolate avenue." At the nadir of despair, with no appar-ent means of escape, Phil kills himself. But sure enough, he wakes up once again, still trapped on February 2. He goes on to kill him-self again and again – and yet each day wakes up, and it is the same day. Phil is condemned to be stuck with himself, facing the ultimate despair that Kierkegaard and Nietzsche describe. But what he first experiences as a living hell he begins to discover, slowly, is in fact a riddle. Phil must figure out how to enjoy the day and how to fill the time constructively. After anaesthetizing amusement has run its course, Phil turns to the kinds of practices that MacIntyre upholds as constitutive of a flourishing life. He studies piano, takes up ice-sculpting, and begins reading poetry. Previously, Phil could only apprehend value in terms of personal exploitation for aesthetic pleasure maximizing; now he is acquiring an appreciation for the intrinsic goods of complex practices.

Focused on these practices, Phil is no longer fixated on the whims of his ego but is instead captivated by meaningful practices. He begins to acquire the necessary virtues so as to make progress and appreciate their intrinsic goods, including patience and persistence. With an abundance of time at his disposal, Phil becomes a skilled artisan. But the concerns noted earlier, with respect to MacIntyre's practices, begin to emerge, especially elitism and the problem of reentry. Fixated on making progress, Phil treats the people he encounters either as means to advance his goals (e.g., his piano teacher) or as obstacles to be avoided. Toward this end, he engineers his day to minimize complications and disturbances that hinder his pursuits. While these practices are an improvement over his immature aesthetic self, they ultimately impede his development and his ability to enjoy the whole day. In spite of his near-perfect foreknowledge of the day, there is always at least one fly in ointment. Phil cannot avoid having to deal with other people unless he remains holed up in his room. The mundane, ordinary life of Punxsutawney, in contrast to the intrinsic goods of piano and sculpting, appears even more drab than before. Though he has become skilled at several worthwhile practices and delights in his new powers, Phil is still living in a Sartrean universe where "hell is other people." At this point, he is not a person of leisure. He has become a striver, setting worthy goals and making progress toward them, but the gift of leisure continues to elude him. He remains haunted by despair.

Love as the Ground of Leisure

Early in this process, Phil's coworker Rita, who he is trying to date, says, "I could never love someone like you. You only love yourself." Phil responds, "That's not true. I don't even like myself"

(Ramis and Rubin, 1992). Extend this sentiment into eternity and you have Nietzsche's eternal recurrence as a living hell – the hell Phil is stuck in. Initially, Phil unconsciously directs his self-loathing outward. He doesn't seem to hate himself; instead, he seems to hate annoying people – which, for Phil, is most people. In spite of his rich MacIntyrean practices, Phil remains caught within Kierkegaard's despair of necessity – resigned to seeing life (apart from his worthy projects) as filled with dreary routine, boring situations, and people that annoy him. At this point, the only viable option that Phil can perceive is the life of a cultured aesthete – disciplining oneself so as to experience the higher pleasures afforded by complex practices.

Essayist David Foster Wallace, in his famous 2005 commencement speech, "This is Water," echoes this theme. Aiming to impart words of wisdom to graduating seniors at Antioch College, Wallace explains how there are large parts of adult life that "nobody talks about in commencement speeches," which involve "boredom, routine, and petty frustration" – or the parts that beleaguer Phil Connors (Wallace, 2009, p. 3). Going further, Wallace paints a picture of a standard nine-to-five workday that the graduates can expect to endure. Wallace depicts, in colorful detail, the typical slog through traffic to the grocery store after a long day at work; a shopping cart that tilts askew as it rolls; other shoppers who seem intent on getting in the way; the dreary Muzak that plays overhead; the insufficient number of cashiers to handle the many customers; the miserable traffic on the way home, and so on. This is exactly the kind of tedium and hassle that Phil Connors seeks, unsuccessfully, to purge from his day.

Wallace's audience is amused at this depiction of an all-too-familiar scene. And, while amused, there is also the realization of how easily we can be rattled by such small-scale frustrations. To the extent that we are unconscious of these dynamics, Wallace notes, we are susceptible to being miserable every time we have to grocery shop because. Wallace elaborates:

> Our natural default-setting is the certainty that situations like this are really all about me, about my hungriness and my fatigue and my desire to just get home, and it's going to seem, for all the world, like everybody else is just in my way, and who are all these people in my way? [This is] the

automatic, unconscious way that I experience the boring,
frustrating, crowded parts of adult life when I'm operating
on the automatic, unconscious belief that I am the center
of the world and that my immediate needs and feelings are
what should determine the world's priorities. (2009, p. 10)

This is the hell that Phil Connors lives in, and a version of the hell
that we recognize. This is essentially how the bored mind is poised
to engage with the world, impeding the possibility of leisurely
engagement.

But what appears to be necessity, Wallace sees as rife with
possibility. Rather than letting this frustration and despair have the
final word, Wallace notes that the "crowded aisles and long checkout lines" give us time to think and reflect – time "to make a conscious decision about how to think and what to pay attention to"
(2009, p. 11). Instead of a default egotism, which sees so very little,
Wallace reveals how we might consider other possibilities, namely
the possibility that "everyone else in the supermarket's checkout
line is just as bored and frustrated as I am, and that some of these
people probably have much harder, more tedious, or painful lives
than I do, overall" (p. 11). If we neglect this, we will surely default
to our bored and miserable selves. Yet instead of the bored self,
Wallace sees the possibilities for becoming a compassionate self. It
is actually within our "power to experience a crowded, loud, slow,
consumer-hell-type situation as not only meaningful but sacred, on
fire with the same force that lit the stars – compassion, love, the
sub-surface unity of all things" (p. 11).

This is the epiphany that Phil in *Groundhog Day* somehow finally lands upon. He has explored aesthetic escapism, suicide,
and self-cultivation. Essentially, he has been fixated on the maximizing autonomy – seeking to rule his own time and circumstance,
including the power to terminate his existence. Like Kierkegaard's
Poet A, Phil recognizes his pursuit of freedom as a form of what
Wallace calls "unconsciousness, the default-setting, the 'rat race' –
the constant gnawing sense of having had and lost some infinite
thing" (Wallace, 2009, p. 10). Instead, Phil discovers what Wallace
describes as true or genuine freedom – "the really important kind
of freedom [that] involves attention and awareness and discipline
and effort and being able truly to care about other people and to

sacrifice for them, over and over, in myriad petty little unsexy ways, every day" (Wallace, 2009, p. 10). It is not fully clear how Phil happens upon this, but he begins to notice the people around him – to take a caring interest in them. What before were occasions for irritation and cause for despair now become occasions for love.

Phil has entered into what Kierkegaard describes as "the realm of love" (1995). In such a state, Kierkegaard explains, "the world—no matter how imperfect—becomes rich and beautiful, it consists solely of opportunities for love" (1995). This is Phil's new world, which also reveals a new kind of freedom. What was a living hell has now become space for boundless leisure. Phil's old freedom, he realizes, was not freedom at all, but rather a slavishness to his fickle desires and dread of boredom. Phil essentially arrives where Bernanos's country priest arrives: a vision of life as suffused with grace. Though fixed within the same day, Phil has now entered a new universe.

The question is, what accounts for such distinctive visions? We can view life as insufferably boring or we can see life as infused with grace. What we do and how we spend our time matters, but how we see and behold what is before us matters more. The protagonist of C. S. Lewis' *The Great Divorce* becomes aware of this when he interrogates the spirit of George MacDonald about the nature of heaven and hell. *The Great Divorce* imagines ghosts in hell granted a sojourn to visit the edge of heaven, if they so choose. Once there, each ghost is greeted by a heavenly spirit, usually someone they knew from their former life, who encourages them to stay and journey further into the heavenly country. Most of the ghosts reject this invitation, holding on to some point of pride or resentment.

Pondering the meaning of all this, and wondering about the meaning of the doctrine of the final judgment (where heaven and hell become permanent states), the protagonist presses the MacDonald spirit, asking if the final judgment is not final, and if there is a way out of hell. MacDonald responds,

> "It depends on the way you're using the words. If they leave that grey town behind it will not have been Hell. To any that leaves it, it is Purgatory. And perhaps ye had better not call this Country Heaven. Not Deep Heaven, ye understand." (Here he smiled at me). "Ye can call it the Valley

of the Shadow of Life. And yet to those who stay here it will have been Heaven from the first. And ye can call those sad streets in the town yonder the Valley of the Shadow of Death: but to those who remain there they will have been Hell even from the beginning." (Lewis, 2001, p. 68)

So then, the protagonist wonders, are hell and heaven just states of mind? Hell, MacDonald retorts, is in fact a state of mind – a "shutting up of the creature within the dungeon of its own mind" (Lewis, 2001, p. 70). Heaven, though, "is reality itself" (p. 70). It is opening oneself to what is – to the horizon that is before us. In *Groundhog Day*, it is through a compassionate move outward that Phil comes to love himself by not thinking about himself at all, by entering into the realm of leisure.

The bored self is poised for misery – "poised for finding ever new occasions to be vexed by the world, by people, by God, by everything" (Kierkegaard, 1995, p. 299). For the bored self, there is, ultimately "nothing new under the sun." Paradoxically, this statement is true of both the bored and leisurely self. The bored self sees through the illusion of novelty as an ever-receding and ultimately empty mirage. The leisurely self, by contrast, finds renewal in repetition. The beauty of life, notes Kierkegaard, is grasping that "life is repetition." Who, Kierkegaard asks, "would want to be moved by the fleeting, the new, that is always ... diverting the soul?" (1843/2009, p. 4). Only "a person who does not delude himself that repetition ought to be something new, for then he tires of it, is genuinely happy" (p. 4). For the bored self, repetition causes despair; for the leisurely self, repetition renews.

The ground of leisure is love. Ultimately, it is love that sustains and supports leisure – that provides the patience and vision needed to endure even the bleakest of circumstances. This is hardly a secret; most people can think of instances in their lives that exemplify this truth. One such instance for me was when my grandmother's health deteriorated. My mother, sister, and I spent countless hours with her, taking her to appointments, consulting with physicians and nurses, and just sitting with her in waiting rooms or at her bedside at her nursing home. In her last six months, as dementia set in, my grandmother could hardly maintain a conversation. Usually we visited on Saturdays and Sundays, arriving to spend time before, during, and after lunch.

It is somewhat embarrassing to recall my 24-year-old self during this time. I remember struggling with the tedium of the nursing home and the hospital. Usually, a television blared *The Price is Right* or a news program in the background. So often I was bored during these visits. Yet, in tension with my bored self was my love for my grandmother – a nurse during World War II, a widow who raised two kids on her own, and an affectionate, sweet grandmother who had the best recipe for rice pudding. We would sit by her bedside, holding her hand. Every so often, I would squeeze her hand three times (a secret signal she shared with me as a child that meant "I love you"). It was this love for her that kept my bored self in check and partially transformed this time into a space of leisure. How I would love to return to that time, and be a better, less-bored self – to cherish and appreciate this extraordinary human being. Boredom, more than a condition that happens to us, is a state of mind that we allow ourselves to indulge in. Leisure is a state of beholding that we must mindfully and lovingly cultivate so that we behold see world as it is – as shot through with overflowing grace and beauty.

REFERENCES

Aristotle. (2013). *The Nicomachean ethics*. (C. Lord, Trans.). University of Chicago Press.

Avildsen, J. G. (Director). (1984). *The karate kid* [Film]. Script. Retrieved February 7, 2022, from www.script-o-rama.com/movie_scripts/k/karate-kid-script-transcript-miyagi.html

Bargdill, R. W. (2019). Habitual boredom and depression: Some qualitative differences. *Journal of Humanistic Psychology*, 59(2), 294–312. https://doi-org.ezproxy.valpo.edu/10.1177/0022167816637948

Benedict, Saint (Abbot of Monte Cassino), & Fry, T. (1982). *The rule of St. Benedict in English*. (T. Fry, Trans.). Liturgical Press.

Berliner, D. C., & Biddle, B. J. (1995). *The manufactured crisis: Myths, fraud, and the attack on America's public schools*. Addison-Wesley Publishing Company.

Bernanos, G., & Morris, P. (1974). *The diary of a country priest*. Doubleday.

Biolcati, R., Mancini, G., & Trombini, E. (2018). Proneness to boredom and risk behaviors during adolescents' free time. *Psychological Reports*, 121(2), 303–323.

Bloom, A., & Bellow, S. (1987). *The closing of the American mind: How higher education has failed democracy and impoverished the souls of today's students (18th ed.)*. Harvard University Press.

Borgmann, A. (1987). *Technology and the character of contemporary life: A philosophical inquiry*. University of Chicago Press.

Borgmann, A. (2003). Albert Borgmann on taming technology: An interview. *The Christian Century*, 22–25.

Brewer, T. (2009). *The retrieval of ethics*. Oxford University Press.

Bridgeland, J. M. (2010). The new dropout challenge: Bridging gaps among students, parents, and teachers. *New Directions for Youth Development*, 2010(127), 101–110.

Brodsky, J. (1995). In praise of boredom. In J. Brodsky (Ed.), *On grief and reason: Essays* (pp. 104–113). Penguin Books.

Bunge, G. (2011). *Despondency: The spiritual teaching of Evagrius Ponticus on acedia*. St. Vladimir's Seminary Press.

Camus, A. (1979). *The myth of Sisyphus and other essays*. (J. O'Brien, Trans.). Vintage Books.

Chesterton, G. K. (1908). *Orthodoxy*. John Lane Company.

Commission on the Reorganization of Secondary Education. (1918). *Cardinal Principles of Secondary Education Bulletin 1918*, No. 35, U. S. Department of the Interior, Bureau of Education.

Crawford, M. B. (2010). *Shop class as soulcraft: An inquiry into the value of work*. Penguin Books.

Crockett, A. C., Myhre, S. K., & Rokke, P. D. (2015). Boredom proneness and emotion regulation predict emotional eating. *Journal of Health Psychology*, 20(5), 670–680.

Danckert, J., & Eastwood, D. (2020). *Out of my skull: The psychology of boredom*. Harvard University Press.

Daniels, L. M., Tze, V. M. C., & Goetz, T. (2015). Examining boredom: Different causes for different coping profiles. *Learning and Individual Differences*, 37, 255–261. https://doi.org/10.1016/j.lindif.2014.11.004

Dante, A. (1995). *The divine comedy*. (A. Mandelbaum, Trans.). Everyman's Library.

Darling-Hammond, L. (2007). Evaluating no child left behind. *Nation*, 284(20), 11–18.

Davenport, J. J. (2012). *Narrative identity, autonomy, and mortality: From Frankfurt and MacIntyre to Kierkegaard*. Routledge.

DePaoli, J. L., Atwell, M. N., Bridgeland, J. M., & Shriver, T. P. (2018). Respected: Perspectives of Youth on High School & Social and Emotional Learning. A Report for CASEL. By Civic *with* Hart Research Associates. Sponsored by The Allstate Foundation.

Deresiewicz, W. (2014). *Excellent sheep: The miseducation of the American elite and the way to a meaningful life*. First Free Press.

Dewey, J. (1913). *Interest and effort in education*. Houghton Mifflin Company. https://doi.org/10.1037/14633-000

Dewey, J. (2018). *Democracy and education.* Myers Education Press.

Dostoevsky, F. (1992). *The brothers Karamazov.* Alfred A. Knopf.

Dubus, A. (1996). *Dancing after hours.* Vintage.

Dweck, C. S. (2006). *Mindset: The new psychology of success.* Random House.

Eastwood, J. D., Frischen, A., Fenske, M. J., & Smilek, D. (2012). The unengaged mind: Defining boredom in terms of attention. *Perspectives on Psychological Science,* 7(5), 482–495. https://doi-org.ezproxy.valpo.edu/10.1177/1745691612456044

Einstein, A., & Pyenson, L. (2006). *Albert Einstein. The collected papers of Albert Einstein. Volume 7: The Berlin years: Writings, 1918–1921.* University of Chicago Press.

Eliot, T. S. (1971). *The four quartets.* Harcourt Brace Jovanovich.

Elpidorou, A. (2017). The moral dimensions of boredom: A call for research. *Review of General Psychology,* 21(1), 30–48.

Elpidorou, A. (2018). The good of boredom. *Philosophical Psychology,* 31(3), 323–351.

Elpidorou, A. (2020). *Propelled: How boredom, frustration, and anticipation lead us to the good life.* Oxford University Press.

"Epiphany" (2021). In Merriam-Webster.com. Retrieved September 19, 2021, from www.merriam-webster.com/dictionary/epiphany

Fermor, P. L. (2015). *The broken road: From the Iron Gates to Mount Athos.* NYRB Classics.

Fitzgerald, F. S. (1999). This side of paradise. Bartleby.com. www.bartleby.com/115/

Flannery, M. E. (2018). *The epidemic of anxiety among today's students.* National Education Association. Retrieved February 7, 2022, from www.nea.org/advocating-for-change/new-from-nea/epidemic-anxiety-among-todays-students

Frankfurt, H. G. (2004). *The reasons of love.* Princeton University Press.

Francis. (2015). *Laudato si'.* Retrieved February 7, 2022, from www.vatican.va/content/francesco/en/encyclicals/documents/papa-francesco_20150524_enciclica-laudato-si.html

Garfinkle, A. (2020). The erosion of deep literacy. National Affairs, 48.

Gary, K. (2006). Leisure, freedom, and liberal education. *Educational Theory, 56*(2), 121–136. https://doi.org/10.1111/j.1741-5446.2006.00007.x

Gary, K. H. (2014). The wisdom of clichés: Liberal learning and the burden or originality [Conference Paper]. Philosophy of Education Society, Portland, Oregon, United States. www.researchgate.net/publication/329518691_The_Wisdom_of_Cliches_Liberal_Learning_and_the_Burden_of_Originality

Gary, K. (2016). Planning for spontaneity or preparing for Kairos in the classroom. Philosophy of Education. https://educationjournal.web.illinois.edu/archive/index.php/pes/article/view/5269.pdf

Gary, K. H. (2017, January). Neoliberal education for work versus liberal education for leisure. *Studies in Philosophy and Education, 36*(1), 83–94. https://doi.org/10.1007/s11217-016-9545-0

Gary, K., & Chambers, D. (2021). Cultivating moral epiphanies. *Educational Theory, 71*(3), 371–388.

Gibbs, P. (2011). The concept of profound boredom: Learning from moments of vision. *Studies in Philosophy and Education, 30*(6), 601–613.

Goetz, T., Frenzel, A. C., Hall, N. C., Nett, U., Pekrun, R., & Lipnevich, A. (2014). Types of boredom: An experience sampling approach. *Motivation and Emotion, 38*(3), 401–419.

Goodstein, E. (2004). *Experience without qualities: Boredom and modernity.* Stanford University Press.

Griffiths, P. J. (2006). The vice of curiosity. *Pro Ecclesia (Northfield, Minn.), 15*(1), 47–63. https://doi.org/10.1177/106385120601500103

Griffiths, P. J. (2009). *Intellectual appetite: A theological grammar.* The Catholic University of America Press.

Heidegger, M. (1927/1962). *Being and Time.* (J. Macquarrie and E. Robinson, Trans.). Basil Blackwell.

Heidegger, M. (1995). *The fundamental concepts of metaphysics: World, finitude, solitude.* Indiana University Press.

Henrickson, J. (2013). Jean-Luc Marion. In S. J. Kristiansen, & S. Rise (Eds.), *Key theological thinkers: From modern to postmodern* (pp. 745–752). Ashgate Publishing Ltd.

Heschel, A. (1977). *Man is not alone: A philosophy of religion.* Farrar, Straus, and Giroux.

Higgins, C. (2011). *The good life of teaching: An ethics of professional practice.* Wiley-Blackwell.

Hillesum, E. (1981). *An interrupted life: The diaries of Etty Hillesum, 1941–1943.* Pantheon Books.

Hitz, Z. (2020). *Lost in thought: The hidden pleasures of an intellectual life.* Princeton University Press.

Hodge, J. (1996). Trainspotting [screenplay based on the novel by I. Welsh]. https://imsdb.com/scripts/Trainspotting.html

Hunter, A., & Eastwood, J. D. (2018). Does state boredom cause failures of attention? Examining the relations between trait boredom, state boredom, and sustained attention. *Experimental Brain Research*, 236(9), 2483–2492. https://doi-org.ezproxy.valpo.edu/10.1007/s00221-016-4749-7

Huxley, A. (1959). *Collected essays.* Generic.

Joyce, J. (1944). *Stephen hero.* New Directions Publishing.

Joyce, J. (1990). *Ulysses.* Vintage Books.

Kafka, F. (1977). *Letters to friends, family, and editors.* Schocken Books.

Kierkegaard, S. (1983). *Sickness unto death: A Christian psychological exposition for upbuilding and awakening* (H. Hong, & E. Hong, Eds.). Princeton University Press.

Kierkegaard, S. (1987). *Either/or: A fragment of life* (H. Hong, & E. Hong, Eds.). Princeton University Press.

Kierkegaard, S., Hong, H. V., & Hong, E. H. (1995). *Works of love.* Princeton University Press.

Kierkegaard, S., Piety, M. G., & Mooney, E. F. (2009). *Repetition and philosophical crumbs.* Oxford University Press USA – OSO.

Kierkegaard, S., Hong, H. V., & Hong, E. H. (2015). *Kierkegaard's Writings, XXI, Volume 21: For Self-Examination / Judge For Yourself!.* Princeton University Press.

Lawson, N. (2020). *Cook, eat, repeat: Ingredients, recipes, and stories.* Vintage.

Lazarides, R., & Buchholz, J. (2019). Student-perceived teaching quality: How is it related to different achievement emotions in mathematics classrooms? *Learning & Instruction*, 61, 45–59.

Leclercq, J. (1982). *The love of learning and the desire for God: A study of Monastic culture.* Fordham University Press.

Lee, F. K. S., & Zelman, D. C. (2019). Boredom proneness as a predictor of depression, anxiety and stress: The moderating effects of dispositional mindfulness. *Personality and Individual Differences*, 146, 68–75.

LePera, N. (2011). Relationships between boredom proneness, mindfulness, anxiety, depression, and substance use. *New School Psychology Bulletin*, 8(2), 15–25.

Lewis, C. S. (2001). *The great divorce*. Harper San Francisco.

Lewis, C. S. (2015). *Mere Christianity*. Harper Collins.

MacIntyre, A. C. (1984). *After virtue: A study in moral theory* (2nd ed.). University of Notre Dame Press.

Mackey, L. (1971). *Kierkegaard: A kind of poet*. University of Pennsylvania Press. https://doi.org/10.9783/9781512804072-007

Mansikka, J. E. (2009). Can boredom educate us? Tracing a mood in Heidegger's fundamental ontology from an educational point of view. *Studies in Philosophy and Education*, 28(3), 255–268. https://doi.org/10.1007/s11217-008-9116-0

Marion, J. (2002). *Being given: Toward a phenomenology of givenness*. Stanford University Press.

May, G. G. (2007). *Addiction and grace*. Harper One.

Mercer, K. B., & Eastwood, J. D. (2010). Is boredom associated with problem gambling behaviour? It depends on what you mean by "boredom." *International Gambling Studies*, 10, 91–104.

Merriam-Webster (2021). Epiphany. In *Merriam-Webster.com dictionary*. Retrieved February 11, 2021, from www.merriam-webster.com/dictionary/epiphany

Merriam-Webster (2021). Leisure. In *Merriam-Webster.com dictionary*. Retrieved August 30, 2021, from www.merriam-webster.com/dictionary/leisure

Merriam-Webster (2021). Jaded. In *Merriam-Webster.com dictionary*. Retrieved August 30, 2021, from www.merriam-webster.com/dictionary/jaded

Murdoch, I. (2014). *The sovereignty of good*. Routledge.

National Commission on Excellence in Education. (1983). *A Nation at Risk: The Imperative for Educational Reform*. U.S. Department of Education.

National School Boards Association. (2011). The case for boredom. *American School Board Journal*, 198(4), 33.

Nhất, H. (1987). *The miracle of mindfulness: An introduction to the practice of meditation*. Beacon Press.

Nietzsche, F. W., & Kaufmann, W. A. (1974). *The gay science*. Vintage Books.

Nouwen, H. (2000). *Clowning in Rome: Reflections on solitude, celibacy, prayer, and contemplation*. Image.

Oakeshott, M. (1989). *The voice of liberal learning*. Liberty Fund. https://doi.org/10.2307/j.ctt1xp3tm1

Orlowski, J. (Director). (2020). *The social dilemma*. Exposure Labs.

Pascal, B. (2018). *The Pensees*. Devoted Publishing.

Percy, W. (1985). *Conversations with Walker Percy* (L. Lawson, & V. Kramer, Eds.). University Press of Mississippi.

Percy, W. (2011). *Lost in the cosmos*. Picador.

Pies, R. (2020). Psychiatry and the Dark Night of the Soul. *Psychiatric Times*, www.psychiatrictimes.com/view/psychiatry-dark-night-soul

Pieper, J. (1990). *Four cardinal virtues*. University of Notre Dame Press.

Pieper, J. (1992). *In defense of philosophy: The power of the mind for good or evil, consists in argumentation*. Ignatius Press.

Pieper, J. (1998). *Leisure, the basis of culture*. Saint Augustine's Press.

Plato, & Bloom, A. D. (1991). *The republic of Plato* (2nd ed.). Basic Books.

Postman, N. (2005). *Amusing ourselves to death: Public discourse in the age of show business*. Penguin Books.

Proust, M. (1913–27). *Remembrance of things past. Volume 1: Swann's way: Within a budding grove*. (C. K. Scott Moncrieff and T. Kilmartin, Trans.). Vintage; French Pleiade (Moncrieff & Kilmartin) edition (August 12, 1982).

Quillen, J. (1991). *Inside Alcatraz from inside: My time on the rock*. Arrow.

Ramis, H., & Rubin, D. (1992). Groundhog day.

Russell, B. (1996). *The conquest of happiness*. W. W. Norton & Company Inc. https://doi.org/10.4324/9780203821053

Scribner, C. F. (2019). Philosophical and historical perspectives on student boredom. *Educational Theory*, 69(5), 559–580.

Scruton, R. (2015). The End of the University. *First Things: A Monthly Journal of Religion & Public Life* (252), 25–30.

Smith, J. Z. (1992). *To take place: Toward theory in ritual*. University of Chicago Press.

Spaeth, M., Weichold, K., & Silbereisen, R. K. (2015). The development of leisure boredom in early adolescence: Predictors and longitudinal associations with delinquency and depression. *Developmental Psychology*, 51(10), 1380–1394. https://doi-org.ezproxy.valpo.edu/10.1037/a0039480

Steel, S. (2014). *The pursuit of wisdom and happiness in education: Historical sources and contemplative practices.* State University of New York Press.

Stevenson, R. L. (1880). Henry David Thoreau: His character and opinions. *Cornhill Magazine.* June.

Strike, K. (2005). Trust, traditions and pluralism: Human flourishing and liberal polity. In D. Carr & J. Steutel (Eds.), *Virtue ethics and moral education* (pp. 224–237). Routledge.

Stutz, C. P. (2017). Wisława Szymborska, Adolf Hitler, and boredom in the classroom; or, How yawning leads to genocide. *Christian Scholar's Review*, 46(2), 127–144.

Svendsen, L. (2008). *A philosophy of boredom.* Reaktion Books.

Taylor, C. (1991). *Ethics of authenticity.* Harvard University Press. https://doi.org/10.2307/j.ctvv41887

The Social Dilemma, Directed by Jeff Orlowski. Producer Larissa Rhodes, 2020. Netflix. www.netflix.com/search?q=social%20dilemma

Thiessen, E. J. (1993). *Teaching for commitment: Liberal education, indoctrination, and Christian nurture.* McGill-Queen's University Press.

Toohey, P. (2011). *Boredom: A lively history.* Yale University Press, p. 33.

Treanor, B. (2021). Gabriel Marcel, *Stanford Encyclopedia of Philosophy.* https://plato.stanford.edu/entries/marcel/

Waldstein, D. (2020). A deeper longing. *The Point*, Oct. 21, Issue 23.

Wallace, D. F. (1996). Shipping out: On the nearly lethal comforts of a luxury cruise. Harper's Magazine. https://harpers.org/wp-content/uploads/2008/09/HarpersMagazine-1996-01-0007859.pdf

Wallace, D. F. (2003). Interview by German television station, 2003, accessed August 31, 2021, www.youtube.com/watch?v=iGLzWdT7vGc

Wallace, D. F. (2007). *Deciderization 2007 – A special report.* Houghton Mifflin Company. http://neugierig.org/content/dfw/bestamerican.pdf

Wallace, D. F. (2009). *This is water: Some thoughts, delivered on a significant occasion, about living a compassionate life.* Little, Brown and Co.

Wallace, D. F. (2011). *The pale king: An unfinished novel* (1st ed.). Little, Brown and Co.

Warnick, B. (2010). Ritual, imitation, and education in R. S. Peters. *Journal of Philosophy of Education,* 43(s1), 57–74. https://doi.org/10.1111/j.1467-9752.2009.00735.x

Weil, S. (1951a). *Waiting for God.* (E. Craufurd, Trans.). G. P. Putnam's Sons.

Weil, S. (1951b). Reflections on the right use of school studies with a view to the love of God. *Waiting for God,* 105. https://doi.org/10.4324/9780203092477

Weil, S. (1997). *Gravity and grace.* (A. Wills, Trans.). University of Nebraska Press.

Weil, S., & Panichas, G. A. (1977). *The Simone Weil reader.* McKay.

Westphal, M. (2003). Transfiguration as saturated phenomenon. *Journal of Philosophy and Scripture,* 1(1), 26–35. https://journalofphilosophyandscripture.org/wp-content/uploads/2018/12/westphal1.pdf

Wheeler, M., (2020). "Martin Heidegger," The Stanford Encyclopedia of Philosophy (Fall 2020 Edition), Edward N. Zalta (ed.). https://plato.stanford.edu/archives/fall2020/entries/heidegger/f

Wilson, T., Reinhard, D., Westgate, E., Gilbert, D., Ellerbeck, N., Hahan, C., Brown, C., & Shaked, A. (2014). Just thinking: The challenges of the disengaged mind. *Science,* 345(6192), 75–77.

Wood, D. (2003). Albert Borgmann on taming technology: An interview. *The Christian Century,* pp. 22–25.

Wraga, W. (2001). A progressive legacy squandered: The "Cardinal Principles" report reconsidered. *History of Education Quarterly,* 41(4), 494–519.

Ziegler, J. (2001). Practice makes reception: The role of contemplative ritual in approaching art. In T. M. Landy (Ed.), *As leaven in the world: Catholic perspectives on faith, vocation, and the intellectual life* (pp. 31–42). Sheed and Ward.

INDEX

Made in United States
Cleveland, OH
23 January 2025

13735651R00087